LIVES OF
UNSTOPPABLE HOPE

SECOND EDITION
REVISED AND EXPANDED

Stant Litore

MORE FROM STANT LITORE

THE DAKOTARAPTOR RIDERS

The Prequels: Gladiators
Book One: Incursion

THE ZOMBIE BIBLE

Death Has Come up into Our Windows
What Our Eyes Have Witnessed
Strangers in the Land
No Lasting Burial
I Will Hold My Death Close
By a Slender Thread (forthcoming)

OTHER TITLES

Ansible: A Thousand Faces
Dante's Heart
Dante's Rose

The Dark Need (The Dead Man #20)
with Lee Goldberg, William Rabkin

&

Lives of Unforgetting
On the Other Side of the Night
Write Characters Your Readers Won't Forget
Write Worlds Your Readers Won't Forget

LIVES OF
UNSTOPPABLE HOPE

LIVING THE BEATITUDES

SECOND EDITION
REVISED AND EXPANDED

STANT LITORE

Westmarch Publishing

2015, 2021

Stant Litore is a pen name for Daniel Fusch.

Cover art by Sarah Menzel.
Cover design by Stevie Schafer.

Illustration on page 32 copyright © 2015 Daisy Dee Designs.

ISBN 978-1-7362127-3-8

A Westmarch Publishing release.

Contact Stant Litore:
www.stantlitore.com
zombiebible@gmail.com
www.facebook.com/stant.litore

Contents

At the beginning of each chapter in this book, you will find a quote from my novels. This is not because I believe that my novels offer the best relevant quotes, but because my novels have been my own dance with God and grief, my own wrestling with the Beatitudes. Through the hearts and voices of my characters, I find a way to cry out to God when the night is at its most silent and its most dark. In this way, I work out my faith in fear and trembling; in this way, I live, day to day, a life of unstoppable hope. May this book inspire you to live a life of unstoppable hope, too.

NOTE ON THE SECOND EDITION

To those of you returning for a second read, thank you. Much has happened in the six years since this book was first published. Inara's story is, well, much bigger. And perhaps my understanding of *hope* is a little deeper. To share the journey and study of these past six years with you, I have added a long closing chapter to the book, "*Phos Hilaron: Six Years Later*," and I hope it will speak to your heart and your imagination. Thank you for reading it.

STANT LITORE

For Tim and Susie Grade,
for Charlie,
most especially for Jan and Jim Buntrock,
and, always, always, for Inara

1. HOPE

Nothing is broken that cannot be remade,
Nothing is ill that cannot be healed,
Nothing captive that cannot be freed.

We must live lives of unstoppable hope.

POLYCARP
IN *WHAT OUR EYES HAVE WITNESSED*

"How can you sing that?" Shimon said suddenly. "How can you?" His hands were shaking. "Everyone's dying. I saw—They're being torn *apart*."

Rahel looked at him in the dark. "Oh, Shimon, Shimon. I am alive, I am alive, I am alive, and my sons are alive."

NO LASTING BURIAL

WHEN MY DAUGHTER INARA WAS BORN three years ago, she immediately began suffering severe seizures. For her first six months of life, we spent as much time in the hospital as out of it, and her mother and I weren't sure she would make it. I sat in that hospital by her bedside, in the cold of winter. It was warm enough in that carefully sterile place, but I *felt* cold. I felt angry. I felt exhausted, and determined. The wind that rattled the windows one night seemed to hurl against the hospital glass all the moaning horror and shrieking of a hostile world.

Now my daughter is improving, and we are on the other side of that time together. Yet those nights by her bed are recent in my heart, and they hurt. I don't know what the past few years have meant, only that the love I now hold for those I call my own is fiercer than anything I have ever felt. I have learned that hope, which I had thought small and delicate like a moth in the night, can be hard as steel, a blade in your hand.

This book is about the Beatitudes, and about my daughter, and it is about unstoppable hope. Wherever I go in my journey with my youngest daughter or in my journey with my God, the Beatitudes pursue me, and I can't escape them.

The Beatitudes are my siren song.

Whenever I read them, whether in our rough but workable English or in the melodic, exuberant Greek, the Beatitudes come to me like a call out of the dark. I stand lashed to the mast of my boat, with the howl of the wind and the crash of the sea against my gunwales, and the Beatitudes rebuke me, telling me I am not living fully, that I am living as a man lashed to a stick of wood on a mighty ocean that might devour me, that a stick of wood is no security. The Beatitudes entice me, telling me to step off my boat into—*onto*—the dark, deep water. To walk across the waves, come what may. They come to me like a seduction. My rational mind knows that should I step over the gunwale, I will be devoured. The sea is without mercy and without compassion; it is too deep and too dark. I know I will not survive that leap, any more than Odysseus would survive flinging himself from his ship to swim toward the sirens who have devoured so many mariners before. I try to stop my ears, but I can't. So I tie myself tighter to this mast. Maybe I can ride out the storm of life; probably that will be futile, but at least I will have this mast, this stick I am roped to, this fragile splinter of sanity in an insane world.

And yet.

The Beatitudes keep calling, calling to me.

They are a quiet, insistent voice in the crash of the storm.

They are honey in my ears. They are wine in my mouth.

They are a hope for the impossible.

Makarios, they whisper, *makarios*.

The most beautiful of words.

Makarios. Blessed.

The Beatitudes

Και ανσιξας το στομα αυτου εδιδασκεν αυτους λεγων

Μακαριοι οι πτωχοι τω πνευματι, οτι αυτων εστιν η βασιλεια των ουρανων.

Μακαριοι οι πενθουντες, οτι αυτοι παρακληθησονται.

Μακαριοι οι πραεις, οτι αυτοι κληρονομησουσιν την γην.

Μακαριοι οι πεινωντες και διψωντες την δικαιοσυνην, οτι αυτοι χορτασθησονται.

Μακαριοι οι ελεημσνες, οτι αυτοι ελεηθησονται.

Μακαριοι οι καθαροι τη καρδια, οτι αυτοι τον Θε ον οψονται.

Μακαριοι οι ειρηνοποιοι, οτι αυτοι υιοι Θεου κλη θησονται.

Μακαριοι οι δεδιωγμενοι ενεκεν δικαιοσυνης, οτι αυτων εστιν η βασιλεια των ουρανων.

Μακαριοι εστε οταν ονειδισωσιν υμας και διωξωσιν και ειπωσιν παν πονηρον καθ' υμων ψευδομενοι ενεκεν εμου. Χαιρετε και αγαλλιασθε, οτι ο μισθος υμων πολυς εν τοις ουρανοις ουτως γαρ εδιωξαν τους προφητας τους προ υμων.

The Beatitudes

And he opened his mouth and taught them, saying:

Blessed are the poor in spirit, for theirs is the kingdom of heaven.

Blessed are those who mourn, for they shall be comforted.

Blessed are the meek, for they shall inherit the earth.

Blessed are those who hunger and thirst for righteousness, for they shall be satisfied.

Blessed are the merciful, for they shall receive mercy.

Blessed are the pure in heart, for they shall see God.

Blessed are the peacemakers, for they shall be called sons of God.

Blessed are those who are persecuted for righteousness' sake, for theirs is the kingdom of heaven.

Blessed are you when others revile you and persecute you and utter all kinds of evil against you falsely on my account. Rejoice and be glad, for your reward is great in heaven, for so they persecuted the prophets who were before you.

2. "BLESSED"

> I've been a slave. I will never again serve anything so small that it can fit in my heart without filling me so full that I can serve only with tears of joy.

> REGINA
> IN *WHAT OUR EYES HAVE WITNESSED*

———————

WE HAVE A LOT OF STRANGE BELIEFS about blessings and being blessed. In this, we are the victims of our language and of languages that came before ours. Language is our oldest and most marvelous technology, the means by which we discover and describe our world and pass what we learn to others. But it is an imperfect technology, one that we are always working, as a species, to improve.

We think that to be blessed is to be fortunate, or happy, or favored by God or the universe. That's the influence of the Latin *beatus*, "favored." But the Greek *makarios* means something quite different. When Yeshua—whose name we have modernized and Englished as Jesus—walked sandalled and dusty through the towns of first-century Galilee and Judaea, whispering, "*makarios, makarios…*" (or more likely the Aramaic *berikh, berikh*), *he* likely meant something quite different.

Our religion, culture, language, and holy texts have all been sifted through Latin, and they carry the sound and scent and flavor of Latin. While Latin is a beautiful language, it is in many ways at odds with the Old and New Testaments. The Romans revered Lady Fortune, whose wheel is always turning. To be at the top of the wheel for a time is to be *beatus*, blessed, favored by the gods.

Μακαριος (*makarios*), the Greek word, has nothing to do with luck or fortune at all. Its root is *mak-,* which means "big." The word communicates "bigness," a life made big. Μακαριος is "enlarged," in the outward-facing sense of "big impact." To live a life that is *makarios* is to live a life that is like a rock thrown into a pond, sending out ripples all around you. It is a life that touches others in big ways. It is a Martin Luther King, Jr. life, a Paul of Tarsus life, a Mother Theresa life. These were profoundly "unlucky" people in the Roman sense, but they lived blessed lives. In the biblical concept of blessing, a blessed life blesses others: it is a big life that makes the lives of others bigger. God tells Abraham that through him, all nations will be blessed, and in the same breath, God tells Abraham to look up at the stars; that is how big, how numerous, his descendants will be! I will make you big, God tells Abraham, and though you, other nations will be made bigger. They will have a big impact on this world in which you walk.

9

To live a *big* life, a life that touches the lives of others: that is to live a blessed life. You don't need to be Martin Luther King, Jr. or Mother Theresa in order to live a blessed life.

My daughter lives a blessed life.

My wife Jessica and my youngest, Inara.

Last week, I spoke with an artist who asked if she could draw a portrait of Inara and a dragon (for Inara is as feisty and as unconquerable as a dragon), and with a writer who has chosen for her pseudonym the name of Inara's childhood friend who didn't make it. Inara's story has touched so many lives during her first three years of life. She has received letters and emails and cards from people who know her only through my writing, or through photos shared on Facebook. During the less dangerous moments in her hospitalizations in 2012, her spontaneous fits of giggles so enchanted the medical staff that the nurses used to sneak her out of the room in the early A.M. hours to cuddle her at our floor's front desk. Nearly everyone who meets her leaves the encounter smiling.

Often, when my wife Jessica has Inara with her at the grocery store or the gas station, some kind and well-meaning stranger, noting our daughter's disabilities, will tell my wife, "You must be so strong, taking care of her," or, "I am so sorry." And though the remark is meant kindly, I have seen such confusion on my wife's face. Yes, Jessica spends five hours every day tending to Inara's therapies and her physical needs. Yes, before we moved into our house, Jessica had to tug Inara's equipment up and down six flights of stairs. But Jessica really doesn't understand how some people assume that Inara must be a burden for her. Inara isn't a burden to my wife; Inara is a beautiful, strong-willed, giggling child who makes my wife's heart bigger, makes her life bigger. Inara's name is inspired by a character on *Firefly* who takes joy and finds serenity in all of life's moments, and her name is Arabic for "radiance" or "blessing." In Inara, my wife and I are not burdened but blessed.

Barak is the Old Testament word for "blessed." It is a deep idea and a good idea. *Barak* originally meant "to kneel and offer a gift of value." To bless originally meant to humble oneself, get down on one's knees, and offer something of high value that would enrich the life of the other person. The one who is blessed by receiving the gift is enriched and enlarged.

So in the older parts of the Tanakh or Old Testament, when God says he will bless Abraham, the visual picture suggested by the word was that of the God of all creation kneeling to offer a priceless gift to a human being whom he loves, a gift that he hopes will enrich and enlarge the one he loves. This might be a familiar image to us, despite the distance across time and cultures; in our own time, consider the bridegroom kneeling to offer his future bride an engagement ring and to ask for her hand. God, like the future bridegroom, is establishing a covenant with Abraham. In God's case, the promised gift is descendants who would have an impact on the world, and a land for them to inherit. God is blessing Abraham by offering a gift of value, and Abraham is blessed by it and enlarged by it.

Similarly, when David in the Psalms says that he will bless God's name, he means that he will kneel and offer the biggest gift he has—himself, his devotion, his praise, his submission—to the God he loves: *I yearn to enlarge your life, God, and to please you, by offering you all that I am.* That is what it is to bless God's name, and it is why we constantly find in the Old Testament the phrase "bless your name" alongside "may your name be great in all the earth!" In the religious poetry of the Psalms, it is humanity's longing to see God blessed and "enlarged" in the earth.

David in the Psalms doesn't think God *needs* him or that he actually *can* enlarge God, but he still yearns to: he still yearns to make God's life better by being with him. He wants God to be pleased and blessed. There is a lot of love/pursuit/marriage language in the Psalms. The bride-groom, in our own culture and romantic literature, may say that he could truly add but little to the life of his glorious bride, yet he yearns to make her pleased and enriched and blessed.

In the Sermon on the Mount—the Greek version that we have—*makarios* is used to talk about what kind of lives are truly made big, what kinds of lives affect (bless) others through their bigness.

———————

Some of you may be reading this little book as part of your own devotions, as part of your journey—or your own freefall—deeper into the heart of God. Since Inara's birth, I have been in freefall, though there is still a long, long way down.

After each chapter in this book, I will offer a brief devotion, a prayer. You are welcome to join me in it, if you would like to. You will find the first of these prayers on the next page.

Prayer

Father, make my heart big, that it may hold more of your love. Father, make my ears big, that I may hear the feelings and the suffering and the fears and the hopes of others. Father, make my eyes big, that I might see the things you see, and not be blind to those who suffer. Father, make my mind big, that I might ask questions and be open to how you are at work in the world. Father, make my hands big, that I might build what you need built and grow what you need grown. Father, be big through me. Make your world big through me. Make others big through me. Father, may your name be big. May your name be hallowed. May your name be blessed.

3. "POOR IN SPIRIT"

The land has become strange to me. I wanted only evenings in my house and Hadassah in my bed. I wanted only my vineyard, only the ripe grapes, the coolness of them beneath my feet, the taste of wine. The long battle with soil and worm is enough for any man of Naphtali. God, you give and you take away, and we are only ashes. We are only ashes.

BARAK

IN *STRANGERS IN THE LAND*

———————

THE WORDS WE CHOOSE ARE IMPORTANT. Yeshua chose his words carefully. He was a man of specific and extreme words.

"Blessed are the poor in spirit." With these words, he opens the Sermon on the Mount. In the Koine Greek translation that survives, the word chosen for "the poor" is the most extreme word possible: οι πτωχοι (*hoi ptochoi*). To be poor in this way—to be πτωχός (*ptochos*)—is to be unclothed, to be utterly destitute and without resources and to know it. It is to be a parent who cannot protect his child, who can only hold her close while she suffers. To be *ptochos* is to be stripped of everything, your skin bare to wind and weather. The man who is *ptochos* lies naked in the dirt, his face pressed to the ground, utterly at the mercy of the one he is pleading to. To be *ptochos en pneumati*—poor in spirit—is to know that you are made of ashes, that you will go back to ashes, that belief in your own sufficiency is a delusion.

It is that delusion—that faith in our bank account, or in our personal virtue, or in the solidity of our house, or in our cunning, or in our family heritage, or in our religious standing—that keeps us from living big, blessed lives. The Emperor cannot be big and blessed in his new clothes, because those new clothes in which he is so confident are nothing more than an illusion. They might blow away at the wind of a child's words. Even so might our house or our religious standing or our bank account or our cunning fail us. Like the Emperor in the story, we all of us stand naked in the cold world, but some of us, experts in denial, choose to believe we are clothed.

The *ptochoi en pneumati*—the poor in spirit—are not blessed because they are poor, because they are naked, or because they are without resources.

They are blessed and able to live big lives because they *know* they are poor, naked, and without resources.

They are the Emperors who have stopped believing in their invisible clothing. Naked, nothing more can be stripped from them. Poor, nothing more can be stolen from them. These are the people who can live day to day, as Mother Teresa did. These are the people who can lie on their side in the dirt without pride or self-imposed stigma, as Ezekiel did, if by doing so they might move the hearts of others, or who can sit night after night beside a loved one who suffers, if by doing so they might offer one sliver of comfort. These are the people who can march in defense of civil rights, no matter what slurs or fists or bullets are hurled at their faces. They have given the day to a higher cause or a higher God than themselves:

> . . . having acknowledged that they were strangers and exiles on the earth. For people who speak thus make it clear that they are seeking a homeland . . . They desire a better country, that is, a heavenly one.

> *HEBREWS 11*

These vagrants, these exiles, these poor in spirit, seek a better country, that is, a heavenly one. They yearn for our world to be more like *that.* They may march, they may weep, they may doubt, they may die, but they will never give up. The call home—the allure and vision of a world where no man is oppressed, no woman is beaten, and no child suffers needless illness, hunger, or violence—is too insistent to ignore.

This place where I stand, *this* place, this place where I sleep tonight, may yet be the house of morning and the house of God. At any moment the eyes behind my eyes may be opened, and I may see angels ascending and descending, touching the crude soil of this exile country and this exile hour with their feet, touching it with heaven. Hoping this, I will fight to make this hour and this place in which I stand worthy of such an appearance. I will never give up, because I am already poor and have no palace to lose. I am ashes ready to crumble in the winter air of this strange land far from home, and I have no fine garments that might be torn from me. I will live hoping at every moment to see the earth at my feet go translucent with the heaven light that is always and ever just about to break through. I am no Emperor; I am just a worshipper kissing this ground on which God might walk.

What will be asked of me?

To carry my daughter across a plain of boiling rock, to save her? I will walk until my legs melt. What are legs to me? I am poor. I can hope God and my fellow human beings will bless me and enlarge me and my family, but I know nothing in this universe can diminish me. I am ash already. I am πτωχός. All I have is hope.

———————

Blessed are the poor in spirit, Yeshua says, "for theirs is the kingdom of heaven."

Prayer

Father, I kneel, naked, before you. I kneel, empty. Empty not like a hole but like a lamp that your light might fill. I have nothing. I cling to nothing. I am utterly poor. Lift me to my feet, if you wish to; I am yours.

4. "Grieving"

The father did not promise a life without pain. Not
without pain. Only that he would weep with us. Only
that his heart would break. Only that he would take
each moment of suffering, each death, each, and hold
it in his hands, and . . . and bring from it something,
something even more beautiful than what was lost. A
forest of cedar grows from a field of ash, and each
seed, each seed must fall to the earth, fall and fall and
crack open and die before it can become a barley plant.

Yeshua
in *No Lasting Burial*

———————

THE GREATEST GRIEF THAT I HAVE KNOWN personally
is that of a father who can do nothing while his daughter
suffers. That is a grief that has torn me open, and the
stitches are still there. But I have seen griefs that are more

wrenching than my own; when our friends lost their daughter, Dahlia Blue, who used to play with Inara when they were both little, I saw their grief, and their parents' grief. Dahlia's grandparents grieved both for Dahlia and for Dahlia's parents, unable to help either their children or their grandchild. To see their grief was like looking in a dark mirror. We mourned for them and with them, and trembled, too, at the thought of what might easily have happened in our own house.

Often, when the night is already old and the children and my wife are already long in bed, and I cannot sleep, I write. Because words are sometimes the only shelter I can build for my family and for myself.

That year, I wrote this, in defiance of both fear and grief:

This is a good life, though one that demands all my resources and will. I have had to adopt a warrior/provider mentality and a certain ferocity, because there is no room for a relaxing of the guard, or laziness, or dwelling too much on needs of my own that are unmet while my wife is ill.

This is winter.

I think life is like this:

In the summer, the days are long and warm and full of life and lovemaking and laughter. The nights are present, but they are brief and hold little pain or fear.

In the winter, it is the nights that are long, and cold and fierce. The days are present, too, but they pass swiftly as a shadow over the grass.

Winter can last long, but that does not mean there will be no more summers. And I sowed many things in the summer that I have since reaped, and that give comfort and sustenance now: a marriage with a woman of astonishing beauty and a giving heart, good friendships, the foundation for a good and meaningful career, and some training in the patience that I now need desperately to endure long nights by my child's bedside or long months while my wife lies ill.

I wish it were summer. But it is not.

I am weary, but I know I am strong enough to endure the winter. And that endurance will not be without enjoyment. It may be the cold season, but my house is warm, and it is full of good books—some of them my own—and with the love of my wife and the laughter of my children, and when they are unwell, the house still sounds with the echoes of earlier joy and rings with the expectation of more joy in the future.

Let the wind howl as it will. This is my home, and these are my own, and I will enjoy my life with them and keep them protected until the days are warm again.

I wrote that, and those are strong words. Yet when I wrote that word *protected*, there was a hole in my heart. I had seen my daughter suffer. There were days when she had dozens of seizures, beginning with partial convulsions and proceeding to grand mal, one after the other, in clusters, as though her body was trying to shake itself apart. And I *couldn't* protect her. All I could do was wait and be there and hold her afterward. I hope that you have never had to suffer that and that you never will. But if you *have*—if you have waited for weeks at a child's bedside, or lost a child, then I will put a pause in the chapter here, because there are no words I can offer. From across these pages, I will sit *shiva* with you. I will sit in silence with you.

STANT LITORE

Some griefs are too deep for words and too terrible for the heart to hold. In the second of the beatitudes, Yeshua speaks of οι πενθουντες (*hoi penthountes*), "the grieving ones." *Penthountes*, like *ptochoi*, is an extreme word. It is not a veiled, stately mourning. One commentary defines the mourning of οι πενθουντες as "a grief so severe it takes possession of a person and cannot be hid." That Greek verb πενθέω occurs frequently in the book of Revelation, in descriptions of the apocalypse, at moments when the ground under one's feet shatters and those who survive grieve in a troubled and collapsing world. The word implies grief over the death of a loved one or over the loss of what you have cherished most, be it a relationship or a once-treasured vision for your own future that now lies in broken shards at your feet. It is the grief that can be met only with silent keening, with rocking back and forth where you sit, continuing to sob long after your tears are gone. The grief that shatters, the grief that empties you out.

———

Yet even that grief dulls like a rusting blade in the end, because we are all captives of time, and time eats everything over which it crawls, everything, even pain. Even if we endure it alone.

And we do not ever endure it alone.

We only think we do.

———

Our child's survival seems to us rare and precious. My wife and I gaze across her crib at each other some evenings in silent wonder and gratitude. I don't have the words to say how stressful and, at times, terrifying Inara's condition has been. In 2012, we truly didn't know if Inara would make it; we just believed in her, stayed by her bedside, fought for her, loved her, and tried to "keep it together." This is also why, late at night when everyone is in bed, I write my fiction so fiercely and fast; it is a way of speaking my pain and my love to the world; it is a way of staring at the possibility of loss without flinching, a way of keeping it together.

I took the night shifts at the hospital. My wife suffers fibromyalgia – a kind of chronic nerve pain that is like the sensation of your skin being on fire, everywhere. Jessica exhausts herself caring for Inara and overseeing her therapies during the day, and she needs every hour of rest I can find for her. So I took care of our youngest at the ER, at the hospital, at the Epilepsy Monitoring Units. For me, those night shifts were harder on my heart than on my body, and I prepared for them in an almost ritual fashion, carving out time before going in (for those stays that were planned) to read to my youngest daughter.

It has become our tradition to read *The Lord of the Rings* or *The Silmarillion*. I discovered quickly—and to my amusement—that Inara prefers the more violent scenes in the books. Perhaps it is some cadence in my voice as I read a battle; perhaps it is something else. Inara, after all, listens to death metal; it comforts her. (I can't say that my daughter's music has the same effect on me.) And when I read her *The Silmarillion*—well, during the Nirnaeth Arnoediad, the Battle of Unnumbered Tears, Inara collapses in hilarity when the dragon squishes Azaghal king of the Dwarves. She giggles herself silly when the Orcs bridge the stream of Rivil with their countless fallen dead, and she squeals with delight as Hurin of the House of Hador hews off the arms of the troll-guard, wielding a great ax two-handed. The smoking of troll-blood on the blade appears to bring her great joy. For my part, those moments of Inara's joy became shield and armor for the long hospital nights.

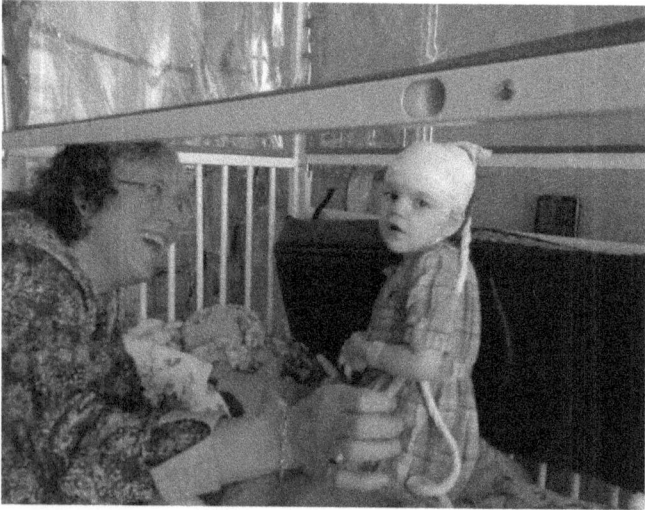

Jan Buntrock, a grief and loss counselor and a dear friend to our family, visited us often at the hospital. Jan and her husband Jim knew when to weep with us and when to laugh with us, and knowing them has made my own heart larger.

I needed what armor I could find. Holding Inara and reading to her while awaiting the return of an endless stream of nurses, I had winter in my heart, and her little smile was the sun. I had never felt so alone. And in those nights I did not know how to call out for help to my father in heaven; I grew up believing that fathers are unreliable. Yet I learned that I *wasn't* alone. My church community brought meals and tears and hugs and sat with me in prayer or sat with me in silence. Coworkers brought meals or took Inara's older sister, River, into their homes for an afternoon to play with other children. Some at the office donated their own paid time off so that I could stay at my daughter's side when things were at their worst. Readers sent kind letters; other writers sent gifts for the children, including what must surely be the world's largest pop-up book. My publisher had four boxes of children's books sent, so that my daughters might have the comfort and strength of entire shelves of stories.

The night the North Pole came to visit a disabled child and her family.

After a flurry of return visits to the hospital in the fall of 2014, my dear friends the Colbys came to our house dressed as Father and Mother Christmas and Chief Elf, delighting River with tales of the North Pole and letting her hold in her cupped hands Father Christmas's magical pocket watch, large as a bowl, which allows Father Christmas to set time *back* so that he can reach all the children before Christmas morning. There are no words for how deeply moved I have been by those who came alongside us during our winter.

"Blessed are the grieving ones," Yeshua tells his listeners, "for they will be comforted."

That word "comforted" is παρακληθήσονται (*parakleitheisontai*), such a rich and beautiful word in Koine Greek. It doesn't just mean to be consoled. It means that someone is "called alongside" you. A *parakletos* is an advocate in your most vulnerable moment, the one who will step down with you into your moment of total grieving, when your grief is so severe that you cannot conceal it or set it aside. An advocate takes your hand and stands for you when you can no longer stand. One of the oldest names for the Holy Spirit, drawn from the book of John, is the *Parakletos*, the Paraclete, the advocate or comforter who visits us in the dark night and reminds us that God is present. So the very name of the Holy Spirit—the name of the active presence of God—is written into this word παρακληθήσονται.

That is a powerful thing.

Having endured a dark moment, we are more able to be there for others enduring dark moments. That is the work of the Holy Spirit, and it is also the work we are each called to do.

In 2 Corinthians, Paul speaks of how those who have been comforted are now blessed in being able to give comfort and strength to others, because they understand others' suffering:

> He comforts (παρακαλων) us in all our affliction, empowering us to comfort those who are in affliction with that same comfort with which we have been comforted by God.

> 2 CORINTHIANS 1

Suffering may not be part of a great Plan in the sense of a precise and pre-ordained divine itinerary for every incident in the cosmos—but the suffering we survive does uniquely equip us to be there for each other. That is how those of us who have grieved are called to live big lives, blessed lives. We are to be paracletes for others who are stepping into the same dark night we have already known. Whether through speech or silence, we can sit with others in their moments of vulnerability, hearing them and holding them, standing for them and with them. By doing so, we witness with our works and with our love.

Inara, dragon-hearted. This drawing was a gift for my daughter from artist Daisy Dee. I never knew how many readers and fellow artists and people admired and loved my family until these last few years. It has meant so much to us, learning that.

Jessica my wife, and River and Inara my children—and I—had a community who drew close around us, who showed up. Not everyone has that. I am very glad we did. I do believe that God is there as Comforter and Paraclete even if no one else is, but God made *us*—creatures of flesh and blood—to be there, to be the incarnated body through which he touches and heals the world. Let's be there. Let's show up. A big life, a blessed life, may not be a march on Washington. It may be a meal brought to someone who is alone in a home for seniors or an arm around the shoulders of a neighbor who is losing her parents. It may be an afternoon playing with children so that their bereaved mother has a few hours to grieve and breathe. It may even be a shared look across a crowded room. Blessed are the grieving, for others will draw alongside them, and they then will comfort others, too.

————————

We made it through our winter.

Prayer

Father, there are people in my community who grieve and ache. There are people who starve. There are people who weep. Help me be alert to them. Gift me with words that heal or encourage. Gift me with silence when silence is needed. Thank you for touching my heart, Father. Thank you for sitting with me, those long nights, even when I scarcely recognized you were there. Thank you.

5. "MEEK"

When a Roman struck a Hebrew across the face, he did so with his left hand, and always with the back of the hand. To turn the other cheek to him … that would be a challenge; the Roman would have to strike with his right hand, or at least with his open palm. To do so would be to acknowledge that he was striking an equal.

NO LASTING BURIAL

———————

OUR WORLD SCOFFS AT MEEKNESS, at restraint, at self-control. Children of the Romantics, we celebrate the unfettered passion, the wild cry on the moor, the lovers sweeping each other off their feet, the ride into the sunset, the man who charges forward and lets nothing stop him. Meekness dismays us; fetters frighten us; we want to remain unbridled.

But an unbridled animal is weaker, smaller, shorter-lived than its domesticated cousin. It has beauty without productivity or security. We are in love with the *idea* of "the wild," even though we do everything we can to wall the wild out of our homes and our cities. We love the idea without understanding what the wild is. To live in the wild is to live in fear.

The Greek οι πραεις (*hoi praeis*) doesn't mean "gentle"; nor does it mean "doormat." It means "tamed." It is the word used in the ancient world for a magnificent war horse or for an expertly trained hound. It is used to describe an animal that has been trained to a particular purpose and is able to follow that purpose unwaveringly, choosing fidelity to that purpose over satisfaction of its own appetites and over accommodation of its own fears. A tamed animal has powerful fears and desires, just as a wild animal does, but a tamed animal does not act on those fears and desires alone. A wild thing may bolt at the approach of a human being, or shy away at a sudden noise, but a tamed horse will wait while its rider mounts and then carry its rider far.

Taming is the act of bringing a living being from a wild state to a domesticated state. I grew up in a farming family, but I am well aware that many people didn't and are at a disadvantage in understanding "taming." A tamed animal is not necessarily a passive animal or even a "meek" animal in the way that we usually understand the word "meek." Anyone who has owned a dog or a horse knows this. Tamed animals may be "subdued" by their master, but they are not necessarily broken-spirited. (They certainly *should* not be, and no one who breaks an animal's spirit deserves to be the owner or caregiver for one.) A German Shepherd who follows the lead of his human master may be quite fierce toward everyone else. We talk about "breaking" horses, but we know now that you can "whisper" horses, too.

The historian Plutarch tells a heart-wrenching story that makes this point better than I could. During a wartime evacuation of the city of Athens, in which the population departs by sea, one man's dog is left behind. Xanthippos' dog sees the boats departing and leaps into the sea, swimming powerfully, fighting the current to catch up with the ship on which his master is a passenger. That is not a passive act by a passive creature. It is a strong, loving, loyal act by a tamed creature.

In the same way, "tamed" people can be as powerful, as active, and as strong as Xanthippos' dog. Meekness is not about weakness. Πραεια ("tameness") is not about a lack of strength but about how your strength is channeled and what guides you in where and when to apply it.

The father-challenge I have is to "tame" my children so that they might be productive adults and not mere ruffians, but to do so without quenching their spirit in the least. My children are creative. They are problem-solvers. River is part diva and part engineer. I am not here on this earth to "break" them, but to "whisper" them, one step at a time, toward adulthood.

And they need taming. They need to understand how to wait in patience for the gratification of a desire. They need to understand how to live more productively by keeping a regular schedule of sleep and work and play and eating. They need to understand that sometimes your body needs the broccoli and not the chocolate. Without this understanding, they would be impaired as adults—ineffective at realizing their dreams or at doing God's work or anyone else's in the world.

To tame them isn't to lock them into cubicles; it is to prepare them to live their purpose, to take all of their creativity, their ferocity, their play, their problem-solving, their laughter, and put it *toward* that purpose. It is not for me to tell them what that purpose will be; it is for me to help them be ready to apply themselves to it, to live big lives, to inherit the earth I and others will leave behind when we depart.

———

To live the untamed life is attractive to us. We tell stories about boys who never grow up and who never forget how to fly—but when we encounter such incomplete adults in our real lives, we often find them entitled, small-minded, even dangerous. It is one thing (a necessary thing) to keep our sense of play and our childlike wonder alive; it is quite another thing to grow up without a sense of integrity, accountability, responsibility, or self-discipline, and without a sense of purpose beyond the satisfaction of momentary appetites.

In contrast, the Christian and Islamic traditions attach great importance to the act of submitting ourselves to God—to realizing our poverty of spirit, that we are utterly without resources, utterly *ptochos* before God. Islam sees prideful self-sufficiency as the root of evil in this world, and Christianity celebrates Yeshua's night in Gethsemane, when he pleaded with God until he sweated blood, and *yet* prayed the prayer of a tamed, disciplined, powerful man: "*Thy* will be done." Catholics celebrate Mary's heartfelt, whispered response to the Annunciation: "Behold, the handmaiden of the Lord"; Protestants make much of Daniel's loyalty in public prayer to his God, attending faithfully to his Master day after day, even in defiance of an emperor's edict and under threat of being cast to famished lions. And in religious households we speak of longing to hear from God at the end of our lives the long-awaited words, "Well done, good and faithful servant."

In a culture that gives men—at best—broken guidance, if any, on how to act and live as adult men, I have been wrestling with πραεια much of my life. It is Inara's time in the hospital that has finally tamed me. Night after night after night, I have stood my post.

If we prove unwilling to surrender, I think two things will characterize our unblessed lives. First, we will live lives in which we cling to our need to control circumstances and others around us; we will clench our hands so tightly about the things that we want to control, that we will live stressed and anxious, miserly lives. We will live wild lives, yes—as anxious and ineffective as wild dogs surrounded by an always hostile environment. Untamed, we will live lives of fear, when we might be living lives of hope.

Living this way, we will not be good hounds. We will bite the hand that feeds us, and we will lash out at others when we feel threatened. We will not be safe to protect and guard those who are weaker or more disadvantaged than ourselves.

We won't be good oxen, either. We will not be able to pull a plow so that the seeds of God's harvest can be planted.

We will not be good horses. We will not be able to carry words of hope to our world.

We may even stay too wild to make good housecats. Too feral even to abandon ourselves in moments of pure, catlike joy and pleasure. Too untamed to bring delight and laughter to our God and to each other.

Many years ago I read the following passage in *The Book of the New Sun*, a science fiction novel by Gene Wolfe, and it has remained with me since:

> We say "I will," and "I will not," and imagine ourselves our own masters, when the truth is that our masters are sleeping. One wakes within us and we are ridden like beasts, though the rider is but some hitherto unguessed part of ourselves.

> GENE WOLFE,
> *THE BOOK OF THE NEW SUN*

So many of us live much of our lives as slaves to our own cravings. Our own desires and fears ride us, beating us forward at a breakneck pace, like cruel riders on hapless horses, until we stumble and break our legs, or crash headlong into other living beings around us, wrecking parts of their lives and parts of our own. Paul describes this well when he speaks of the nature of sin:

> For I do not understand my own actions. For I do not do what I want, but I do the very thing I hate . . . I have the desire to carry out what is right, but not the ability to carry it out. For I do not do the good I want, but the evil I do not want is what I keep on doing . . .

> ROMANS 7

We all know this story. We all know the damage we do. When we live untamed lives, seeking our own head and galloping where we please unchecked and undirected, we become the creatures of our habits, rather than the children and agents of our God.

Proud as I am, I have learned the joy of standing my post. I have learned why the psalmist cried out:

> For one day in your courts is better
> Than a thousand elsewhere!
> I would rather be a doorkeeper
> in the house of my God
> than dwell in the tents of wickedness.

> PSALM 84

The beatitude of "meekness" beckons me to remember the creative or destructive power of my choices. Nothing is more powerful than choice. I might live as an unwilling slave to my own cravings, or I might live as a willing and treasured servant dedicated to a high calling and a high God. Rather than toss my head like a willful stallion, I might wait, my strength reserved, and be certain of my direction; I can allow God space to enter my life and nudge me. I am *not* God, and living as though I am will not make me free.

Prayer

Father, I have long been a wolf ravening the edge of your forest, when I might have been your hound. I have long been a deer fleeing each of your footfalls, when I might have been your steed, carrying you down the corridors of cedars and into a world that yearns for you more than a deer yearns for the brook. Tame me, Father. Make me yours. Make me strong that you might wield me. Make me peaceful that you might heal me, and others through me. It is exhilarating running wild along the ridges, the wind in my fur; and yet—and yet, Father—I would rather eat from your hand and serve you in making your homestead in the cold winter of this universe than waste my footprints in the snow of a thousand hills. I have howled at the moon, and now I will stand watch at your door.

6. "HUNGERING AND THIRSTING FOR JUSTICE"

No nation, though it have decorated tombs taller than mountains and all the world's perfumes—no nation can be called great if some of its people starve, or are sold to beds in other cities, or are forgotten, or sacrificed to the dead to make a few men feel safe.

DEATH HAS COME UP INTO OUR WINDOWS

———————

THERE IS A HUNGER IN US; living in this world of cancer and prejudice and a thousand evils both named and unnamed, we starve for justice. The fourth Beatitude speaks of οι πεινωντες και διψωντες (*hoi peinontes kai dipsontes*), "those hungering and thirsting." We usually make this into 'better English' by translating it as "those who hunger and thirst," but when we do, we risk losing the power and nuance of the

Greek participle. This hungering and thirsting for δικαιοσύνη (justice, righteousness) is continual, so much so that it is a core, driving characteristic of those doing it. It becomes an adjective to describe who they are; their hungering and thirsting for δικαιοσύνη is just as essential to who they are as being poor in spirit. They are "those hungering and thirsting for justice," those who live and act in a state of holy discontent.

———————

Holy discontent (a phrase I borrow from pastor Susie Grade) is something with which we aren't familiar enough in America. The media inundate us with images of global and local suffering. We either stop watching or we spur ourselves into a state of constant but passive outrage. The sight of a malnourished child or news of a stoning in another country no longer moves us. We become numb. Desperate to remain content, we become complacent and inactive. We no longer live blessed lives, merely blind ones. God looks at the world and sees every bleak moment of suffering and every small moment of joy. Yet we train ourselves to walk with our eyes closed.

Missionary Bob Pierce famously wrote on the flyleaf of his Bible: "Let my heart be broken with the things that break the heart of God." This prayer is as necessary as it is dangerous and inconvenient. If we are to live blessed lives, if we are to live lives "worthy of the calling to which we are called," then we had better *feel* that call. We need to *stay* sensitive to the injustices around us. We *need* to be discontent. We need to *value* being discontent. And that doesn't mean discontent over traffic or your parking space or the size of your office. It means discontent over what makes *God* discontent: children orphaned and unloved and unprovided for; society's "untouchables" shoved to the side and permitted to starve there, out of sight; widows and the ill neglected; the hungry unfed; the thirsty left without water; the grieving left without comforters to sit by their side. If we ever want to be truly full, if we want to be fed on God's food—rather than just numbly unaware of the extent to which we are becoming spiritually famished—then we need to hunger and thirst after justice, continually, day by day. How has it come to pass that we observe everything in our world through media and memes, as though we are watching a thousand movies and commercials at once? How has it come to pass that we are mere spectators to the sufferings of others?

Hebrews 11 gives an eloquent description of the holy discontented, who are continually crying out for justice without ever seeing that justice fully realized:

> These all died in faith, not having received the things promised, but having seen them and greeted them from afar, and having acknowledged that they were strangers and exiles on the earth. For people who speak thus make it clear that they are seeking a homeland . . . They desire a better country, that is, a

heavenly one. Therefore God is not ashamed to be called their God, for he has prepared for them a city.

HEBREWS 11

Of such people as these, God is not ashamed. These are people whose hearts are broken at what breaks God's heart:

By faith Moses, when he was grown up, refused to be called the son of Pharaoh's daughter, choosing rather to be mistreated with the people of God than to enjoy the fleeting pleasures of sin.

HEBREWS 11

Witnessing the pain of others and the injustices of the society of which he was a part, Moses risked all that he had.

Blessed are the people who have a founder like that.

He and so many others like him desired a *better country*, a heaven-country, and they acted on that vision. They looked around them at the world, discontented, feeling as out of place as sojourners and exiles in a strange land, and found themselves hungering and thirsting after justice.

———

Justice.

Let's talk about justice.

The Greek word used in the fourth beatitude is nuanced and powerful, and it's worth looking at for a moment.

49

Δικαιοσύνη (*dikaiosunei*) – literally, "that which is approved" in the eyes of God. It is traditional to translate this as "righteousness" to emphasize that it's what God sees as right and good (as opposed to what human authorities proclaim as moral and right), but we have lost a lot of the resonance of that word "righteousness" in our culture, in part because we only use it in contexts noting hypocrisy, as when we refer to "the self-righteous," those who find themselves right and just in their own eyes. Δικαιοσύνη is about rightness and justice in God's eyes. It is a specific way of looking at justice—the kind of justice that when God sees it, he approves, just as God approved when he looked upon the Creation and saw that it was good. Δικαιοσύνη is human beings acting in ways that make their Father proud.

Jacques Derrida suggests that justice is the name we give to an event for which we are always waiting. We are always hoping that justice is about to arrive, that it is about to be served. We write law in order to try to bring about the event of justice, but there is always a gap between law and justice, a remainder, something or someone who gets left out. This is because law deals in universals, in absolutes that can be applied to each situation with uniformity. But justice is only served when the needs of each individual person in each individual situation are satisfied. This is why, in the gospels, whenever the Pharisees or the priests confront Yeshua on a point of law, speaking to him in universals or in generalities, Yeshua responds by citing a specific situation or telling the story of a specific person. Asked about the Sabbath, he tells the story of David feasting on consecrated bread on the holy day. It isn't that there's "an exception to every rule"; it's that every person and every situation *is* exceptional. Justice is about the individual's plea, where law is about the general rule, and these two will always exist in tension. Law may be the best we can do to try to summon justice to the situation, but if we are those hungering and thirsting for justice, we will rarely be satisfied by law; we will suspect, as Martin Luther King, Jr. does in his Letter from the Birmingham Jail, that not all laws are just. We will be restless, ravenous, quick to question the gap between the law we have made and the justice we yearn for.

Hurriya in my novel *Strangers in the Land* is one of those who gets "left out" by an impersonal and imperfect law. Hurriya challenges Devora, the highest judge in the land, with these words:

> You think the Law is a pact with your God, a pact with others of your People. But it's not just a pact. It's an answer. You have rules for everything. But it's not the rules that matter. It's that you *want* to make them. You want to answer the suffering you see in another woman's face. You want to give her safety, or justice, or comfort. That's what matters. That's why you have your Law, why you love it. But when you sit in decision at your olive tree, or on this horse looking at this burning town, you have to find the right answer to the suffering you see. Your fathers in the desert found the Law, found that answer. So it guides you . . . But you still have to find the right answer to each face you see.

HURRIYA

IN *STRANGERS IN THE LAND*

Οι πεινωντες και διψωντες την δικαιοσυνην, those hungering and thirsting for justice, are those who are not satisfied with a general rule that neglects individuals' needs, those who are not content with the status quo, those who are not only discontented but *ravenous* for change when they look upon the world and see wrongness instead of rightness, when they see human beings acting unjustly and abusing one another:

> For Zion's sake I will not keep silent,
> and for Jerusalem's sake I will not be quiet,
> until her righteousness goes forth as brightness
> and her salvation as a burning torch.

> *ISAIAH 62*

Longing to rest in God's arms, in religious communities we often forget our hunger, our thirst. We may be too quick to dismiss those who are blessed with a restless, discontented, famished desire for justice. "Why can't you just forgive and forget?" one community mutters. "Don't worry about these bad things happening, they are all part of God's Plan," a second community pollyannas. "If you've received injustice, you probably did something to earn it," a third community pronounces.

Yet Yeshua never said any of these things.

Yeshua said, "Blessed are those hungering and thirsting for justice."

———————

The second half of that beatitude is: "…because they will be filled."

I want to be careful. I don't think this should be read as a platitude. I do not believe that God wants us to see life as a Hallmark card. I think he wants us to see the world's injustice and the incredible agonies of human beings for exactly what they are: a travesty, a train wreck, the ongoing rape and torture of everything life was meant to be like. Our world—and you do not need to look to starving children in some other country to see it, you can see it if you look in your own city; I see it in my city—is filled with injustices that will make us cry until our bodies can't bear the pain of it, if we look around us for one moment with truly unlidded eyes.

We must never cheapen the reality of human suffering with platitudes. The response to a world that knows rape and cancer and child soldiers and ethnic cleansing and human trafficking and senseless deaths and broken marriages cannot be: "It's part of God's plan."

That is *not* what we are asked to put our faith in.

What we are asked to put our faith in is a promise about the future that has been made to us by the Maker of all things, by the One who gave birth to something as vast and full of unexpected beauties as the universe. Creation is what God does. And the promise we have from God is this: that he will continue creating. That no matter what happens in our world or no matter what havoc human beings wreak on their own lives or on each other, he will always find a way to create new life and new joy. We are asked to trust that this is who God is, to put our faith in his creativity and his love and his commitment to us and to his universe. We are to trust that no matter how dark a situation seems, there will come a beauty and a joy—"new heavens and a new earth"— so wonderful and so fulfilling that the joy will eclipse the suffering that preceded it.

And as with the world, so with any individual human life. No matter how much a man or a woman might wreck their life, if we are willing God might transform us from the inside. We can be made new.

For those who live with a fierce hunger for justice, with a thirst that tears at the heart—for those who hunger and thirst, there is a specific promised blessing. Χορτασθήσονται (*chortasthesontai*), Yeshua says: we will be fed, we will be fully satisfied, we will be "engorged."

That Greek verb χορτάζω (*chortazo*) means 'I gorge myself' or 'I fatten myself.' Say the word χορτάζω and feel it in your mouth: it is actually a really funny word. It has a very funny sound. Χορτάζω! In the Middle Ages, religious scholars frequently contended that Christ had no sense of humor and that though he was recorded as having sweated and wept, he was never recorded as having laughed. I think these scholars saw the words of Yeshua as humorless because they read them in Latin rather than Greek. It is difficult to say "Χορτάζω! I engorge myself! I burst! I am coming apart, I am so full!" without a grin.

Χορτασθήσονται is a remarkable promise, a ridiculous promise, a wonderful promise, if we have the courage to believe it, if we have faith even the size of a mustard seed. Yeshua is speaking this promise to human beings, who know suffering. In the first century, he is speaking it to people living in poverty within an oppressive empire where their most basic rights might be revoked at any hour. Yet he is asking them to trust so deeply into God's love that they can laugh with him. God has seen the end of the story, and it is worth laughing about, though we who live our lives in the middle chapters, in a broken world that we see "through a glass darkly" cannot imagine how an ending that would provoke delighted laughter could be possible.

Blessed are those who hunger and thirst after justice, for they will be *gorged full* of justice.

They will see *so much* justice, so much rightness.

They will be so full that all they can do is loosen their belts and laugh before sitting back and closing their eyes in a dozy contentment.

That's how much justice and rightness God plans to bless us with.

Hungry for justice and rightness in the world? Yeshua asks on the Mount. Well, my Father is going to have a *banquet*. And all of you here on the street will be welcome to the table. And at that banquet, the world is going to become so full of justice that you will be engorged with it. You will be fully, fully satisfied.

———

Even as I wrote the first draft of this chapter, Inara began having what looked like gelastic seizures—fits of seizures that manifest as bouts of hysterical, uncontrollable giggling. Afterward, she would often slump, exhausted, or even black out. This would happen four or five times a day, and it threw us into a panic of medical tests and anxious vigilance.

I stopped writing this book for many months.

My heart had been torn open. The injustice of it ate at me. Inara had been largely free of seizures throughout 2013; she was beginning to pick up new skills and recover lost ground. The thought that she might lose all of that again, perhaps even be plunged back into long weeks at the hospital—it was like watching the sun die into dusk without any hope of dawn.

Yet I did hope.

My wife and I awaited, fiercely, the results of the tests. And early in 2015, Inara's epileptologist called us with a startling answer, in fact the best of all possible news.

This past year, Inara has *not* been having gelastic seizures as we had feared.

She has been having honest giggles, but due to her delayed development, her laughter consumes her entire body; she loses all control of her body when she laughs, and the blacking out is actually from physical exhaustion. Much as an elderly person might lose control of their bladder while laughing hard, Inara loses control of everything.

Inara also has a very low exhaustion threshold compared with you and me. This is why she can't eat normally yet: she hasn't been able to develop the necessary muscle tone for her jaws and after trying to eat for a bit, she's literally too exhausted to continue or to do anything else. (Inara receives 85% of her nutrition through a G tube.)

So apparently, when something strikes Inara as funny, her laughter consumes her and burns what energy she has and then she either blacks out or just slumps and lies listless for a while until her body recovers. We thought we were looking at post-ictal exhaustion, the fatigue-state that follows a seizure. But no. Inara literally laughs herself into exhaustion.

The doctor thinks Inara, who is partially blind, sometimes sees a shadow from the corner of her eye or a funny blurry shape, and that sets her off. "She'll find something hilarious that you can't see in an empty room," her doctor tells us, "and she knows it is the funniest thing in the universe."

I have a very happy daughter. As we've confirmed that we're not looking at seizure activity—and haven't been since 2013—the doctor has approved dialing Inara's dosage back a bit and continuing to watch her. But she and her team have consensus that Inara is no longer having seizures.

My wife and I are vastly relieved. And, once I can start breathing again, I'll probably also be very amused that Inara finds things in life so hilarious that sometimes she faints from the sheer humor of it!

I have become so accustomed to hitting the high-adrenaline, get-ready-to-fight button whenever something happens with Inara that can't be explained and that looks dangerous … but now it looks like my wife and I can actually breathe for a while. When I first received this news, I was so thankful and relieved and exhausted and happy, I thought *I* might pass out.

Sometimes—just sometimes—we get a glimpse of that banquet of justice and rightness that is yet to come. Sometimes, we get a sense for what it must mean to push back from the table and groan, "*Chortazo!* I am full! I am so, so full!"

Inara lets nothing stop her. Here she is working on the muscles that will someday help her walk. In 2012, the doctors told us she would never be able to stand. She proved them wrong. Inara lives a life of unstoppable hope.

Inara painting—on a day when she has almost no eyesight.

I am still trying to let that sink in.

I cannot begin to express how much this promise, this blessing, astonishes me and moves me. In the rare moments when I feel that I glimpse or grasp this blessing—as when a starving man catches the scent of a banquet and realizes the door is open and not barred—when I see my daughter giggling until she blacks out, or making music on an iPad tablet with her toes, when I see her painting with her fingers and knees and feet on a canvas my wife has provided her, painting all the poems she cannot speak, I want to laugh, too. I want to laugh hard with Inara. I want to laugh hard with God.

Prayer

Father, may my heart be broken by what breaks yours. May I be moved to act. May your better country come. May your will be done. May we receive from you, day by day, the sweet bread of justice, of rightness, of a world made well and whole and sound.

7. "MERCIFUL"

When you see another's face—the face of a child, or another woman, or the face of someone hungry or hurt—their eyes, they look back. They look at you. They ask your love, they ask you to hear their crying and know that you and they are both alive, and some day you may be hurt, you may be hungry. It may be your child carried dying in your arms. When I look at you, you look back. Only the dead don't look back.

HURRIYA

IN *STRANGERS IN THE LAND*

———

Ελεος, ελεος (*Eleos, eleos*) . . . LIKE MANY GREEK WORDS, it is beautiful. It means mercy—or compassion—or what people who spoke English long before us called "ruth." *Eleos* is what happens when we see another in tears and we cry, too. *Eleos* is what happens when our hearts are bruised at the bruises we glimpse on others' faces. Erasmus describes the "merciful" as people who, "through brotherly love, account another person's misery their own; who weep over the calamities of others; who, out of their own property, feed the hungry and clothe the naked; who admonish those that are in error, inform the ignorant, pardon the offending; and who, in short, use their utmost endeavors to relieve and comfort others."

———————

A hunger for justice, for δικαιοσύνη, might provoke varied responses in us. Anger, certainly. Perhaps violence. Maybe in our ravenous need for things to be *right*, we turn riot and destroy homes, shops, or lives around us. This has happened in history many times, and will happen again. Justice too long delayed can create explosive pressure.

Riot is one response.

Another is *eleos*. Mercy. And forgiveness.

This is not a passive choice. It is a fierce willingness to let ourselves be changed, that the world might be changed through us. It is a refusal to drink the poison others pour for us—the poison of resentment, or unrestrained fury, or bitterness, or hate. An eye for an eye and soon the entire world is blind, Gandhi warns. Cling too tightly to our grievances and leave our past unburied, and it will rise to devour us.

———————

"Blessed are the merciful," Yeshua says, "for they will receive mercy."

Do acts of mercy engender more acts of mercy? I do not know—I doubt—but I hope. I hope.

The philosopher Emmanuel Levinas speaks eloquently of the demand of the human gaze, the meeting of the eyes at which two people recognize in each other their essential kinship, their shared humanity. In Genesis 1 (in Hebrew), we find the phrase *tzelem elohim*: each person is made in the likeness of God, whether male or female, Caucasian or Latino, Christian or Muslim, old or young. In Genesis 2, we find God breathing into the nostrils of the first human being. And in the words of one of the living novelists I most admire:

> The breath of God was his breath yet though it pass from man to man through all of time.

CORMAC MCCARTHY
IN *THE ROAD*

When we hear another human being breathing, do we hear the breath of God? When we see another human being with pain in her eyes, do we see in her eyes God's pain?

Gandhi's project of *ahimsa*, nonviolent resistance, was about pressuring the oppressor to meet the eyes of the oppressed. That is, to acknowledge their kinship, that shared humanity, in the hope that once you recognize that kinship, no response other than ελεος—mercy—is possible.

Is there anyone whose eyes you have refused to meet, lately? Or anyone you are more comfortable considering in the abstract, as a statistic, as one of "those people," anyone you'd find it uncomfortable to see face to face?

Sometimes, ελεος is about taking the time to recognize people, to hear them and get to know them—people that others have forgotten or shoved aside.

In Alpharetta, Georgia, a beautiful town outside Atlanta, there is an academy for troubled youth. Last winter, the owner and her sister shared with me (anonymously, without names attached) some stories of the teens that near broke my heart. These are good teens trying to turn their lives around after being in some bad places. Some have been involved in drugs; one young girl was prostituted by her brother. Heart-wrenching stories. When I visited, I could see in their faces—some of these kids don't believe they have the right to have dreams. Some wear ankle bracelets; some have been sent to that school by a judge. All have been told, in various ways, that they are of no worth.

During the winter, my publisher and I sent the teens copies of *What Our Eyes Have Witnessed,* which is a novel about people in intense poverty in one of the ancient world's most awful ghettos—the Subura in Rome—who choose to live lives of unstoppable hope. It is a powerful story and I chose it carefully; the main characters include an apostle running a soup kitchen, a rescued sex slave, and a rich kid who is overwhelmed by the poverty he sees and who tries to get involved. The story is also full of zombies. The teens at the academy love zombie stories. Atlanta, GA is zombie fandom central: the home of *The Walking Dead*.

When the owner's sister invited me out to speak to the teens, I started by reading a scene where Father Polycarp faces the dead; the teens were riveted. I'm told that I'm a very performative reader; I'm very, very into it. The owner and her sister, for their part, told me how good it was to see their kids engaged.

Afterward, the teens and I talked for quite a while. We talked about zombies, about being an author, about what it's like growing up, about being brave and having dreams. I met wonderful kids here in Atlanta—good kids, who just need someone to believe in them.

One of the teens asked me, "Are you from Atlanta?"

"No." I explained that I live in Colorado.

"Are you here just to talk to us?" He looked baffled.

"Yes," I said. "I came out here just to talk with you. That is the one reason I'm in Atlanta."

The message: I value you. I believe in you.

That, I hope, is a powerful message.

When I signed books for them, the owner told me that many of these teens don't have much of *any*thing that is theirs. To have this book by an author they've met is meaningful.

Another of the teens saw my email address in the book. He asked if he could email me. "You can," I said.

I hope he will.

And this morning, I heard that one of the teens had told the owner's sister that *What Our Eyes Have Witnessed* was the first book he had ever read all the way through.

I told the owner that this visit she and her sister were thanking me for was a gift *they* had made to *me*. To see an entire room of teens who were so into one of my stories, who had been moved and puzzled and then motivated by it, to know that for a few of them at least, the story had made a difference, to see their eyes light up in considering new possibilities, that is a powerful gift. When I told them that you just have to find that one thing you really enjoy and pursue it and don't let anyone tell you that you can't, one of the young men grew excited. When I explained how much I love reading to people, and how I read to my wife each night to distract her from her chronic pain so that she can sleep, one of the young women, her eyes lit up. It is possible that this young woman had never before considered that a man could treat the woman he was with that way; that kind of relationship may not have been part of her world. Now, I hope, she knows it can be.

The teens I met in Atlanta are struggling, but I realized, seeing their faces, that they just need someone to believe in them—as Polycarp believed in Regina in *What Our Eyes Have Witnessed*. Regina, a rescued sex slave, becomes the deaconess of an underground church in ancient Rome, the weaver together of many lives. Despite a past of suffering and misery, Regina lives a life of unstoppable hope in that book. I believe these teens can, too. They just need someone to tell them that no matter what happened yesterday or what their lives have been like, they're allowed to live a life of hope, allowed to dream, and read, and believe that tomorrow could be different.

Meeting them has touched me, and I will not forget them.

———

I am haunted by society's forgotten children—the children in sweatshops in Pakistan, the children on the streets of Los Angeles, the eyes of children on the border between the US and Mexico—*children*, held in what are essentially kennels and cages. When we fail to meet the eyes of others, when we fail to respond with mercy, when our hearts are hardened like the hearts of Pharisees, when we insist on seeing others in categories rather than as individuals and as fellow human beings—when we see them as enemies, as slackers, as "the 47%," as debtors, as delinquents, as terrorists, as dirty foreigners, as sinners, as, well, take your pick—it is the young who suffer most. We visit all our crimes upon our children, and we make our children and others' children suffer for our own hardness of heart.

> If a people could forget the pain in the eyes of children, they could forget God. And if a people could forget God, they could forget the words she gave. If they could forget the words she gave, they could forget the pain in the eyes of children.

DEATH HAS COME UP INTO OUR WINDOWS

Our exodus, our road out of the violence of our shared past—a violence that we must take responsibility for cleaning up after, because it won't clean itself up without our intervention—our road out of that dark wood is *eleos*, mercy. As yet, I know of no other road.

Prayer

Father, soften my heart. Soften my heart. Soften my heart.

8. "PURE IN HEART"

They considered each other. Then she did something he did not expect. She let the blanket slip from her shoulders, let it settle to her feet, gently as feathers. For a moment, she held her arms across her breasts, then let them fall to her sides. She lifted her chin, though her face burned. She let him see her, all of her, her beauty and her bruises. This gift of herself. Her father might strip her or beat her, but he could not take this from her: her right to open her heart and her body to one whose heart called to hers. Koach held his breath. All his life, he would remember this moment. His first sight of her. The memory would be holy to him. As though her rooftop were the place where God touched the world and created beauty.

His loins stirred for her, yet his face was wet.

Whether he wept for her, for himself, or for them both, he couldn't have said. His hand trembled as he lifted his fingers to the clasp of his own tunic. He kept himself fully clothed at most times, even in his mother's house; he couldn't bear the way others looked at him when his deformity was visible. But he could not hide it now, could not conceal it when this young woman had unclothed all of her bruises, risked everything to be seen by one other. He kept his movements slow, his heart loud with his fear. It took some work, with only his one hand and not his mother's to aid him. But at last his clothes were in a heap beside him, and he stood naked on the roof, the air cool on his skin.

NO LASTING BURIAL

THE "PURE IN HEART," οι καθαροι τη καρδια (*hoi katharoi tei kardia*), Yeshua tells us, are blessed—for they will "see God." They will see God in the faces of others, in the trembling of a leaf on the wind, in the holy and awe-inspiring beauty of their lover's body, in the small act of compassion of a man paying for another's coffee at the counter. The pure in heart are awake, alert as an antenna to God's presence in the world, alert to the hearts of others. Koach, pure in heart that night on the roof, has no shame in being naked or in seeing Tamar naked. Their intimacy is deep and pure: no veil between their bodies or their hearts, and no longer any sense of a need for one.

What purity of heart I may have, I have because of my daughters. They teach me to look at a dirtied world and see its potential for cleanness and beauty; to look at a new scene and see its potential for wonder; to see another weeping and respond with an innocent concern and desire to help. When Inara cries in her crib, whether for attention or because she is afraid or because she is frustrated, River runs across the house shouting, "Check Inara, daddy! Check Inara!" That is purity of heart: to see another's need and respond with the desire to *get help*. Not with embarrassment, not with any abashed desire to withdraw, not with any need to silence the other's pain, and not with an assessment of how to use that other's vulnerability. That is purity of heart.

To see God in the faces of others.

There is a misconception in our culture that to be *katharos* – "pure" – is to be separate. Entire religious communities stress reading only certain fiction, listening to only certain music, and associating only with certain people. Nothing could be *less* pure or less biblical: Yeshua himself associated with—had dinner with—people of all walks of life and of all shades of social standing: tax collectors; prostitutes; priests; zealots urging terrorist acts against Rome; an *Iscariot*, that is, an assassin wielding a curved knife against Roman soldiers or citizens; unlettered fishermen; housewives; diseased lepers; the disabled; legislators; soldiers; the proud and the humble alike. If one is to suppose that Yeshua was pure in heart, then pure in heart cannot mean separated and cut off from one's neighbors. The pure in heart "see God" not because they keep themselves blind to their neighbors or because they choose not to see particular movies or hear particular cuss words. The pure in heart see God in every moment in which God stands—which is every moment. They see God in every human face, and are moved to love and compassion.

Katharos—pure—means not "unmixed" but "cleansed." Unworthy thoughts have been sifted out of the mind, unworthy desires have been cleaned or scraped out of the heart. The word originally conveyed ritual cleansing. It is not what you see but what you permit to inhabit the house of your heart that makes you impure. It is not what you take in from the world around you but what you put out into it that makes you unclean. It is not what is done to you but what you do that makes you filthy. This is why it is such a severe injustice to shame a victim of rape or abuse as though she is impure or unclean; it is why Augustine, weeping, wrote letters to the nuns of Rome, raped and abused during the sacking of the city, to tell them that, in his eyes and in the eyes of God, they remained virgin and pure in heart.

Our culture mocks feminists for insisting that a woman should be able to walk into a party naked without "asking for it." But our culture is wrong. Our culture is afraid of its own impurities of heart. Tamar stands naked on her rooftop and for Koach, this is a holy moment. He sees the beauty of her body and the beauty of her heart, and he is moved not to use her but to heal her. Being "pure in heart" has nothing to do with what or who you are looking *at*, or sharing a meal with, or making love to. Being pure in heart has to do with how you respond to what or who you see, with how you speak, how you act, how you embody God's presence in the world. If men were God's hands and feet, if the men at that party were pure in heart, then seeing the woman walk naked into their room, they would see someone desirable, yes, but they would see also a person, a daughter of God—and would be moved to *treat* her as a daughter of God. It is not her body that is an issue to the men in the room, but their own blindness. Our blindness as human beings is cortical, as my daughter's blindness is cortical: it is not about what we see but about how poorly our brain interprets and makes sense of what we see. My daughter looks at the world and sees little pieces of it, blurred; so, too, we look at those around us and see only pieces of them. How beautiful would be our world—and how blessed—and how blessed each of us would be—if we could see God when a woman walks naked into a party. If we could be moved almost to weeping by the beauty of the men and women and children who surround us each day.

———————

When I wrote the character Yeshua in *No Lasting Burial*, I wrote him as a man truly pure in heart—a man who could see and hear the hearts and the pain of those around him. Everyone whose voice he hears appears to him to be both indescribably beautiful and worthy of love *and* to be in the most terrible pain. He hears the cries of our hearts, of our loneliness. It drives him almost mad. He sees God looking back at him from the eyes of everyone he meets, demanding his response, demanding that he see in them not someone to assess or use or judge, but someone who is his kin, his neighbor, someone into whose body has been breathed the breath of God.

What do you see when you look at another human being?

Polycarp asks this of a gathering of people hiding in the Catacombs beneath ancient Rome:

> "All our lives, we feed on what leaves us hungry, drink from what leaves us thirsting. Because we are always left hungry and always thirsty, we begin to think that those visible objects of our hunger are what we need most. A loaf of bread, a pouch of coins, the respect of others, success, a woman's body, or a man's. Or even a person or a thing from times past, something lost and remembered that we crave. But it is not so. These are not what we need most. Our hunger thieves us from our true selves. Like a violent fever, the hunger eats away mind and spirit. In the end, everything that we truly are is gone. Only the hunger remains. Even other men and women are no longer anything but food to us, meat for our desires and obsessions. Then we are lost."

WHAT OUR EYES HAVE WITNESSED

What do you see when you look at that impoverished woman ahead of you in the line with four bawling children at the grocery store? Do you see a dirty immigrant to be feared and driven out, someone who might compete with you for food and funding? What do you see when you look at your coworker? Someone to use in some way to advance yourself? Perhaps someone attractive, to be used sexually? Perhaps someone who might use *you*, someone to fear? As Polycarp warns us, we often look at other human beings as either eaters or as something to be eaten. But people are not food. What we think of that woman ahead of us in the grocery line or that attractive, intimidating coworker has little to do with what we are seeing and everything to do with what is already living in our hearts.

———————

My daughter's vision improves a little, each month. Some mornings, she can catch a glimpse of me only out of the corner of her eye, and she'll tip her head to the side and peer at me that way. Other mornings, she can gaze full at my face and laugh with me (or possibly at me: every child knows how ridiculous adults are…). Those are good days.

She is training her brain to process more of the visual stimuli that her eyes receive. We, too, might improve our vision. It may take time, as it does for my daughter. But it is our hearts that are blind, not the organs of our eyes. There is no irreparable physical damage that keeps us from seeing God looking back at us out of the faces of our fellow human beings made in his likeness. Let us not avert our eyes from anything or anyone; let us instead clean our hearts.

I want to walk down the street today and see God.

I want to stand in line at the grocery store and see God.

I want to hold my wife naked in our bed and see God.

I want to sit at the bus stop by a man who reeks of alcohol and urine, and see God.

I want to see God everywhere.

I yearn for God that much.

I yearn for a clean heart. I yearn to see a world clear and almost violent in its beauty and depth and color, not the fuzzy, blurred, gray world through which I usually walk. The eyes of my heart need vision therapy, need healing.

Prayer

Create in me a clean heart, Father. Open the eyes of my heart. I want to see you.

9. "PEACEMAKERS"

Peace was more than stillness. More than sleep. More than numbness, more than the absence of conflict.

Peace was consolation and wholeness. Peace was two men breaking bread together, forgiving an old quarrel. Peace was a mother holding her infant up to its father for the first time, or a mother opening her eyes to greet her child after long illness. Peace was two lovers in each other's arms after a long, good night. Peace was an open door and a wall torn down.

No Lasting Burial

WE TELL OUR DEAD TO REST IN PEACE, we ask for peace and quiet, we "make peace" by ending a battle, because our "peace" is a descendant of the Roman *pax*, the absence of conflict, order, silence. But Roman *pax* was a false peace and an oppression for many. The Greek is *eirene*, which means "woven together," like a thousand colored threads in a brilliant tapestry. The Hebrew is *shalom*, which means "full-flourishing." In a perfectly ordered *pax*, in a stable *status quo* with no conflict, people may find themselves stacked on top of each other in orderly castes and not woven together at all; lives may be prevented from full-flourishing because privileging the absence of conflict above all else keeps issues from being resolved, reconciled, or forgiven.

Traditionally the first ancient verb that a student of Koine Greek learns is λυω (*luoh*), which means both "I destroy" and "I loosen," a pairing that can confuse at first—until you realize the extent to which weaving was a potent metaphor for the ancient Greeks. The Fates weave our lives as one might weave a cloth or a tapestry, and at the end of our life, Atropos snips our thread with her lethal shears. The spine in the back is imagined as a cord to which all the threads inside our body are woven. When a warrior falls in battle in epic poetry, "his limbs are loosened." Once that spine is severed, all the threads fall slack, and a human body drops as limply as a snipped puppet.

Even as the limbs of the body are woven to its trunk, so too are communities woven together, in the Greek imagination. Thus Paul speaks to early Greek churches, urging them to weave themselves to one another in love, to allow nothing to loosen them. When the threads of a beautiful coat of many colors are loosened from one another, the coat frays and then falls apart. To loosen is to destroy; to weave is to make beauty. Penelope, waiting for Odysseus's long-delayed return, weaves a funeral shroud by day and unweaves it by night. When we first encounter Helen of Troy in *The Iliad*, we find her at her loom. Weaving is a potent metaphor in the ancient world—in part because it takes so much time and effort and talent. A hand-woven rug with an intricate design might well take a young woman in the hills of Anatolia a year to complete. And how easily a thing that took a year to make might be loosened and unwoven.

Peacemaking—ειρηνοποιειν (*eirenopoiein*)—is not just a pretty word; to the Greek mind, it is the name for a kind of craftsmanship, a work of intentionality and labor. It is not merely the ceasing of conflict but the integration of people in the warp and weft of a shared community. In the novel (and film) *Cloud Atlas*, the ex-slave Sonmi 451 says, memorably:

> Our lives are not our own. From womb to tomb, we are bound to others. Past and present. And by each crime and every kindness, we birth our future.

DAVID MITCHELL
IN *CLOUD ATLAS*

Bound to others: woven together. By our every act, we are either weaving or unweaving our world—by strengthening or fraying the relationships in it. Blessed are the peacemakers, Yeshua preaches, because they will be called the "children of God," children of the great Maker, the great Weaver-together of lives.

————————

Peacemaking is the hard work. We may love the ideal of diverse colored threads woven into a tapestry, or that of of diverse biological parts—eye, ear, hand, foot—woven together into one body, but our human record with weaving people together is astonishingly bad. We are tribal, hot-blooded creatures, and our distant biological ancestors scampered away into the foliage at loud noises or the scent of a predator. We have, each of us, a little of the prey-animal left in our blood. When we encounter something or someone different, someone who surprises us, we might respond with hunger—*this is something to consume*—or with fear—*this is a threat that must be fled or attacked*—or with wonder—*this is something strange that I should look closer at, and get to know.* Our wonder and our curiosity might help us weave our lives to others whose color or appearance or beliefs are different from our own, but the other two reactions—hunger or fear—lead us to rend and tear others, or to pull our own threads away in a hasty, panicked fraying. And those reactions are more common than wonder, at least in jaded adults. A change management expert told me once (I haven't verified the statistic) that eighty percent of people fear change and difference and their first reaction to it is hostility or resistance. Only twenty percent welcome change; only twenty percent see something or someone different and find their curiosity ignited, find themselves drawing near to learn more. As fearing, hungering creatures, we frequently unweave our world.

This is River, carrying an invisible baby bird in her cupped hands.

Weaving is a creative, not only a practical, art. There may be a clue in this. To relinquish our own habits of hostility and fear and weave our lives to others' in peace requires both patience and creativity. Confronting a situation that triggers old fears or makes us angry or unsettled, we typically imagine that our situation has only one or two possible resolutions. In reality, it probably has many, and it is only a failure of imagination that keeps us from coming up with a new approach, a new settlement, a new way to relate to others.

River is a peacemaker. At preschool, she helps distribute toys to make sure all the other children have something to play with. When two other young ones are squabbling, she steps in and sorts it out gently. "Share," she says, "share." (When did we adults forget how to do that?) When her mother is in bed with fibromyalgia, River digs out Jessica's stethoscope and pressure cuffs (my wife is a CNA) and gives her mother a medical checkup. "Mommy, I be your doctor-helper. I make you feel better," she says. We've taught River that if she hurts her knee or tumbles over a step, she can just get back up on her feet. But River doesn't have any contempt for a child who sits down on his butt and cries. She just waits patiently for her friend to finish and stand back up. River is an extremely social child; she wants to be woven to others. She approaches other children of different race, class, gender, and fashion sense with curiosity, not trepidation. "Hi! What's your name? I'm River." She organizes other children for a game, not by bossing them but by the sheer pull of her enthusiasm. I admire her fiercely. I wish I were half the peacemaker she is. River teaches me God's heart. She teaches me that weaving people together is a possibility, however jaded or bitter I may feel today. She teaches me to hope.

Prayer

Father, weave me to my children. Weave me to my wife. Weave us to our community, our friends, and to those we fear and dread. Make us the into most beautiful of garments for you to wear, many-colored and flashing in your light. Weave us together in peace, Father. Whisper in my ear this week, at every choice: let me see how I might weave or unweave relationships each day. Help me to fasten rather than fray, to tie rather than tear, to repair rather than rend. Teach me, Father, to help you make the world beautiful.

10. "PERSECUTED"

He knew all the stories. His grandfather had given them to him when he sat between the old man's knees as a child. It was a comfort, though, to hear them again. To call them to mind. All these stories that made him more than just a vintner and more than just a man who carried a spear whom other men were willing to follow. More than just a man who lay dying. The stories made him one of the People, who would never die.

STRANGERS IN THE LAND

HOWEVER DARK THE LONG NIGHT of waiting by my daughter's bedside in the cold hospital room, I have never been alone in my wait. Woven to each other, we are none of us alone. We are part of a larger story. Whether we think of that story as tragic and dark or bright or as some mix of the two almost doesn't matter; what matters is that we are part of something much larger than ourselves, something that has gone on long before we were here and will go on long after we are gone:

> Blessed are those who are persecuted . . . for so they persecuted the prophets who were before you.

> *MATTHEW 5*

The writer of Hebrews offers the same word of consolation to the first-century house churches who must often meet in secret:

> And what more shall I say? For time would fail me to tell of Gideon, Barak, Samson, Jephthah, of David and Samuel and the prophets—who through faith conquered kingdoms, enforced justice, obtained promises, stopped the mouths of lions, quenched the power of fire, escaped the edge of the sword, were made strong out of weakness, became mighty in war, put foreign armies to flight. Women received back their dead by resurrection. Some were tortured, . . . they were sawn in two, they were killed with the sword. They went about in skins of sheep and goats, destitute, afflicted, and mistreated—of whom the world was not worthy—wandering about in deserts and mountains, and in dens and caves of the earth.

> *HEBREWS 11*

It is a strange comfort, perhaps, that this letter offers to these early people in hiding, people fearing for their lives or the lives of their children or their loved ones. Yet it is a mighty comfort. Not a single one of us is alone or insignificant, because we each walk among a mighty crowd of fellow witnesses to the world's pain, fellow exiles, fellow grieving ones, fellow men and women who, poor in spirit, meek, striving to make peace, have gone on hungering for justice and for restoration and for *rightness*. We walk alongside David and Deborah, Samuel and Samson, Martin Luther King, Jr. and Harriet Tubman, alongside men and women who have struggled and won, and among men and women who have struggled and lost. Their struggle is ours, and ours, theirs. We are all on pilgrimage, all of us exiled together and walking the long walk toward a better country. And that can be a source of hope! Of unstoppable hope. Not of the weak, delicate butterfly hope I once imagined, but of sword-blade hope, the hope you carry at your side and wield when demons or dark monstrosities leap into your path. Strong as steel though slender, that hope is what we use to cut our way through.

———

Because there *is* hope. I speak of that hope in Christian terms because that is my story and my tradition, the one I know and live, the one that daily transforms and reforms my heart. But a Jew or a Muslim or—albeit in very different terms—a Buddhist would affirm, too, that we are right to live lives of unstoppable hope, hoping for not only restoration but rebirth and resurrection. Hoping that from the fertile ashes of any desolation, a paradise can rise:

> For I consider that the sufferings of this present time are not worth comparing with the glory that is to be revealed to us. For the creation waits with eager longing for the revealing of the sons of God . . . For we know that the whole creation has been groaning together in the pains of childbirth until now.

> *ROMANS 8*

Blessed are those who travail, Yeshua tells us. Blessed are those who suffer, who are persecuted, who are reviled when they seek justice—for theirs is yet the kingdom of heaven. The better country they seek is out there, and the birth for which they labor will come. Some day. And they are blessed because they are members of a greater kingdom and chapters in a greater story, and they are not alone in laboring for that new birth. People throughout all of human history labor and yearn and laugh and weep along with them.

That is what the name I have taken—Stant Litore—means. It is from the *Aeneid*. As Troy is burning and Aeneas leads the survivors fleeing toward the shore, someone ahead of them shouts: "Hurry! Hurry! The ships stand at the shore (*stant litore puppes*)! The anchor is already drawn up! Hurry! The ships are here to take you away!"

As far as the refugees know, this is the end of their world; their world is nothing now but smoke and ash. What they *don't* know is that once they embark on those ships and cross the sea, they are going to found Rome. They have a mighty and amazing future ahead of them that they can't even imagine.

Even when everything is ash, we have no way to know what will come with the morning. But we can hope. The ships stand at the shore, and every moment of destruction is a moment of embarkation, too. What happened yesterday both does and doesn't matter; we will need to clean up after yesterday, but tomorrow is still a new, unknown day.

I was there when Inara was born, and River before her. I held my wife's hand as she labored; I saw the first, wide-eyed look that she exchanged with each of our moist-eyed, beautiful, newborn daughters. I will never forget that, nor the sound of her soft weeping or the exhausted warmth of her smile the first time she held each of them close. I will never forget her panic at Inara's first seizure, nor my own. I will never forget the thirty hours she labored, gasping and exhausted, working with God to make a new life at the cost of great pain and fear. I will never forget the nights we stayed awake watching over Inara, when her seizures would roll through her, one after another after another, when no medications would slow them. I remember the brief fear for my Jessica's life, and the long fear for my Inara's.

———————

"Blessed are you when you are persecuted," Yeshua tells his first century audience. The Greek word used in the surviving text, οἱ δεδιωγμένοι (*hoi dediogmenoi*), means those who have been harried and hunted right down into a hole in the ground, like a hare with hounds at its heels. It is a frantic word, a word that connotes a long and exhausting night of pain and terror with no safe refuge or harbor anywhere and only the prospect of brutal suffering and death when at last you are caught. It is a terrible word. It is an injustice that the Greek language even *has* such a word, or needs one; it is a horror of our history that such an experience exists, that we live in a world where pastors in West Africa throw acid into the faces of small children to exorcise them; where millions are extinguished like candles in the gas showers of Shoah, the Holocaust; where an earthquake might kill a city or a cancer kill a young woman; where a woman might die in the very effort of bringing into our dark world one new life.

I growl in my heart when I hear the word "persecution" tossed around on the air waves or waved like a banner. In our country with its many luxuries, many of us have become small people with small and even contemptible concerns. We think we are being "persecuted" if someone glares at us from behind the cashier, or objects to a slogan we wear on our shirt, or if we are prevented from putting a Nativity set on public property. And when others call out to us for justice that inconveniences us or infringes on our privileges, we accuse *them* of persecuting *us*. This is the "persecution" we imagine when we are living small lives, lives of unblessing; this is not the "persecution for justice's sake" that Yeshua suggests comes with a blessed life, a big life.

———————

I pause here to confess that I do not know how to write this chapter.

I have not endured persecution as some of my friends who are of color or who are LGBTQ+ have. And I don't know from personal experience what it's like to be an undocumented college student who might be deported, alone, to a country she doesn't know, all of her life ripped away in an instant, or to be the parent of a child in a border camp, a child physically torn from your arms, to be deported then with the belief (and the probability) that you will never see your child again. That is a horror I can barely imagine.

I only know what it was like seeing Inara born, seeing her suffer, seeing her fight to live and thrive, my brave, dragon-hearted daughter. I have known the sense of being hunted to the ground by enemies that I can neither name nor see, of being helpless to defend my child. I do know that. *That* is a story I can share. I know that the moment of childbirth is a sacred moment where suffering is translated to joy, sacred because it has been shared by billions of people. And the moment when an illness—an illness that the doctors cannot even *name*—lapses and ebbs away like a retreating tide, leaving behind only broken memories of broken nights—that is sacred, too. Because millions of people, suffering small evils or great, have also suffered and hoped for a morning that either did, or didn't come. That is an experience I share with my entire species. Telling the story of it is sacred. It is like kindling a flame in the dark and looking out across a wasted landscape of blasted trees and volcanic rock and seeing across the miles and across the years a thousand thousand other kindled flames, like so many stars fallen to earth and yet undoused. Still burning in the night.

———————

I wrote what follows some time ago to a friend who has suffered and survived and overcome things I can barely imagine, and who, like me, suffers periods of doubt and deep depression. I wrote these words for her, but I share them here for you also:

> Good actions can have hard consequences, yet it is the good actions that make us people who we want to be, even if our world is not always a world we like. The trouble is that we expect it to be a world that we like, and it isn't, it is a broken, messed-up world. But we can live it with people who matter for as long as they're with us. We can give our heart into things that matter to us, regardless of how many other people they matter to or don't. And that's really all we can do. Live, love,

make great art, cherish the people we're with while we can, and raise hell. The God who moves beneath the universe and calls us to live and love... is living and loving through us and is proud of us. Our value is inestimable, because we are bright burning stars in the middle of a vast dark that wants to put us out.

I don't think you took any wrong road. I think sometimes there are no roads. The trees are dark and thick; you burn brightly nonetheless, and we are all glad that you do.

I do not yet know how to write this chapter because I don't know *your* life. I don't know where you have been hunted or persecuted or harried, or whether you ever have. I don't know if you have ever been spat upon for the color of your skin or for your sexual orientation or for your beliefs or for anything else. And I don't know if you have ever wept at a daughter's bedside, or a dying parent's.

So how can I presume to speak words to your heart?

I am only lifting a brand from the fire and waving it in the night, as if to say: Here I stand, and I see *your* fires out there in the dark, too, and I see God's presence blazing in all of these flames.

And seeing your fires out there, this is what I want to tell you: We can live lives of unstoppable hope.

We must.

We are all pages in the vast story that God is reading, that we and God are writing together. The road is dark and the wind is shrieking: yet we will walk hopefully and fiercely. We will remember the story we are in. We will remember our song in the night; we will rejoice and be glad; we will be salt-seasoning and light in the dark. Let the winds howl as they will; the storm may slay us, but it will never, *can* never unmake us or defeat us. Be still, waves. Be still, wind. We—my readers and I, and David and Moses and Gandhi and Buddha before us, and who knows but perhaps Clone 776-A5 and Martok of New Mars and as yet unimagined saints after us—will walk across this sea. And some evening yet, in this life or the next, there will be a shore, and a better country. We will keep walking toward it together, through one night or a thousand. Many waters cannot quench love; neither can the floods drown it. Nor will anything quench us. Loving, living, hoping, creating, woven together and weaving ourselves together, to God and to each other, we will never be quenched. You and I, we are going to live blessed lives, big lives, lives of unstoppable hope.

11. WALKING ON WATER

I have reached the roof of the world. No one told me
it would be this beautiful.

YEPTHA'S DAUGHTER
IN *I WILL HOLD MY DEATH CLOSE*

———————

I AM UNTYING MYSELF from the mast. At least for today,
for this moment, for this prayer. Tomorrow, I may need to
undo these same knots again. But today, here, now, the siren
song of the Beatitudes--of God's still, small voice—is loud
in my ears. And I believe that this sea that seems so waste
and wild is actually so full of fish that I might walk across to
the shore on their backs. I have only to trust, and step out
of the boat. I have only to live a life of unstoppable hope, a
big life, even if it should kill me. My little Inara lives such a
life. How can I fail her by doing less? I will carry her in my
arms and I will walk out across these waves, the surface of
the water wet beneath my naked feet. The alternative is

simply not viable; maybe I am a fool to hope, but if in the past a fool carried an account of resurrection into the rotting heart of the Roman Empire, if another fool chained herself to a carriage's wheel so that the makers of laws could not ignore her, or if two fools we imagine could carry a Ring together up the slope of Mt. Doom, surely I can carry my daughter through any nightfall. Surely I, too, can live restlessly, relentlessly, as such a fool.

> For the foolishness of God is wiser than men, and the weakness of God is stronger than men.

> 1 CORINTHIANS 1

I believe that. I hope it. More fiercely than I yearn for the sunrise.

I hope.

Two most beautiful words. Words that can change worlds. I hope.

I hope.

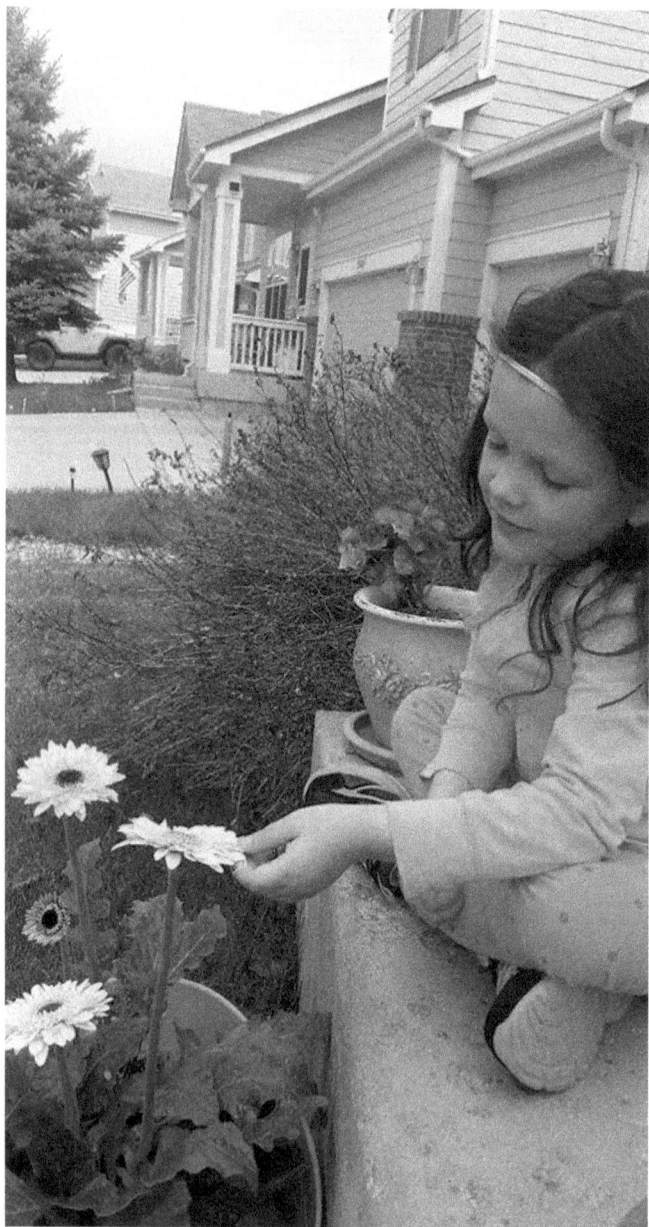

Benediction to the First Edition (2015)

This is not a gray world.

May your days be alive with the electrifying colors of God's presence and wonder.

May you look up and around you even in the midst of your burdens.

May you look for God's love in the faces around you, in the falling of rain, in the sound of footsteps in snow.

May you take in the colors of the life God gives you until your eyes and spirit ache with them.

May you be as a bride seeing in every hour the face of her Beloved.

May your wonder make the colors visible to those who walk with their heads down.

May your surprised joy and your devotion make the voice of God audible to those who walk with their pain loud in their ears.

12. *PHOS HILARON:*
SIX YEARS LATER (2021)

You have hope, daughter. That's what you have. Hope. It's the best thing that ever was or ever will be. Spun from stories, stronger than medicine, older than this world. Hope is what braids our lives together. Hope carried our people between planets and hope carries us through the red rain and hope will carry you.

ANNIKA NIGHTWATCHER
IN *THE DAKOTARAPTOR RIDERS*

———————

IT HAS BEEN SIX YEARS since I published the first edition of this book. I return to it now to add this closing chapter because recently, during this past year, geneticists have taken a fresh look at Inara's exome and have identified the gene that has caused my daughter's suffering. We learned of it a few days ago—and the timing was remarkable, as we had just returned from a devastating episode at our local hospital. Inara's seizures, after years of staying controlled by medication, had come back, and she nearly died; she was lifeflighted by helicopter from our local emergency department to the most advanced ED and pediatric intensive care unit in the state. Several times that night, she stopped breathing. Her heart rate crashed. I saw my daughter turn blue. I will never forget that.

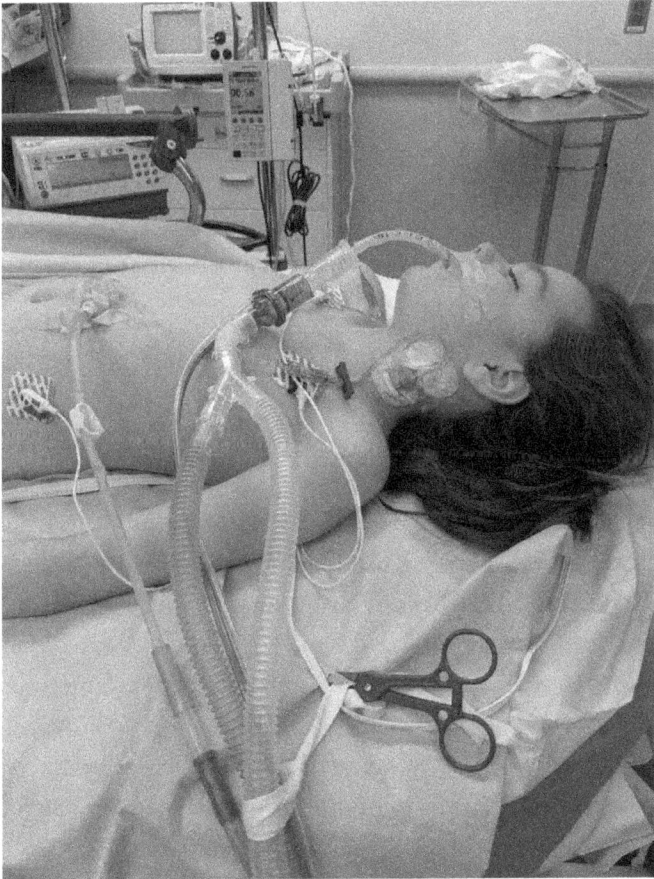

By the grace of God and by considerable skill and a passion to preserve life, the doctors brought her back. She was lethargic for some time, unresponsive, my feisty little dragon who bites people as a way to say "hello," who paints with her feet, who learned last year how to climb on top of tables and perch there and screech like a hungry wyvern, my nine-year-old daughter—here she lay, barely aware of the world around her, and for a time hardly seeming to care.

For days at the ICU, I sat at her bedside watching her recover, caring for her, too exhausted even to acknowledge my own terror—that the beast we thought Inara had beaten was back, that it would always be lurching behind her waiting to seize her, that she would have to fight it all her life, after all. That she might not make it, and there might be nothing we could do. That the beast still had no name.

———————

Well, it still doesn't have a name, but after our call with the geneticists this week, it does have an *origin*. That origin is the gene RHOBTB2 in the 14th chromosome, only recently identified. Researchers Staub, Konrad, et al. just published a paper on that gene and on Inara, entitled "Missense Variants in RHOBTB2 Cause a Developmental and Epileptic Encephalopathy in Humans, and Altered Levels Cause Neurological Defects in Drosophila." The paper documents how a mutation in this gene has affected ten children in the U.S. whose exomes have been sequenced, including our Inara:

Epilepsy manifested in all of the individuals reported here within the first 3 years of life (between the first week and ninth month in nine of ten individuals). Seizure types were variable and included focal dyscognitive and generalized tonic-clonic seizures… five individuals experienced status epilepticus… Neurodevelopment was severely impaired in all individuals through a lack of or delayed mobility and speech abilities. Developmental stagnation was reported in one individual and regression was reported in five, correlating with the onset or worsening of epilepsy… Although birth measurements appeared to be normal, postnatal, progressive microcephaly was common, and postnatal growth retardation occurred in five individuals.

These are definitely Inara's symptoms—symptoms she shares with a handful of other children. The gene RHOBTB2 is part of the genetic code having to do with the nervous system; the error in the gene (one incorrect letter) prevents the correct amino acid from being produced, and causes problems in the way messages get relayed from brain to body and from body to brain; at least, that is my limited, layman's understanding of it. My Ph.D. is in the humanities, not in genetics, and I am intensely, deeply grateful to those researchers whose passion for the genetic language in which our bodies are written mirrors or exceeds my own passion for the languages in which our hopes and dreams are written, and by whose passion and study lives are saved. The missense variant in RHOBTB2 is like a loose circuit in a switchboard; it's a breakdown in the body's communication system. It's why Inara seizes.

The researchers report that the seizure activity these children experience proves difficult to keep under control and causes stroke-like symptoms. That has certainly been the case with Inara. Finally, the paper includes photos of five of the other nine children who have this error in gene RHOBTB2. Looking at their faces this week, I cried. Inara is no longer alone in the world. She is unique in her own way; she is rare, because she has survived what could easily have killed her; but she is no longer *alone*.

The geneticists and neurologists who met with us to share their findings told us about two children in our own Colorado, two out of the other nine. (The fact that three have been discovered at the same hospital tells us that there are many more out there—it's just that no one has ever known before now to test for errors in this gene.) One of the children is near Inara's age, but the other is very little. My heart aches for those parents; Jessica and I have given the doctors permission to connect us, if the other parents wish it. I remember what it was like in those first few years, with the doctors as much in the dark as we were, fighting for Inara's survival with no clear idea what was going on. That is a terrible place to be.

In those years, when we spent nearly as much time *in* the hospital as *out* of it, we hunted vigorously for answers. Frequently, we were offered tentative diagnoses, best guesses—*if not this, it is very probably this; if it isn't Rett Syndrome, it must be Angelman; if it isn't Angelman, it must surely be Malignant Migrating Partial Seizures of Infancy (MMPSI)*—and that made for a nerve-wracking odyssey through the medical literature. Jessica and I sailed uneasily between the Scylla and Charybdis of varying fears for the future, different horrors the future might hold for our daughter. I recall our relief when we thought it might be MMPSI, because most children with MMPSI die during their first sixteen months, and Inara had made it to three years of age by that time. That diagnosis would have told us: *She has made it through the worst. We are now on the other side of that night.* There was a new light in my eyes, and in my wife's. But, a few months after I published the first edition of *Lives of Unstoppable Hope*, when the initial results came back from Inara's whole exome sequencing, we learned it wasn't MMPSI. It wasn't *anything* that geneticists knew how to identify at that time; no cause for Inara's condition had been found. There was no diagnosis, no prognosis; no one knew what to expect. We were plunged right back into the dark, yet again. But—we had our daughter. At least for that day, she was alive, she was laughing. So we took joy in that, and we hoped. We hoped.

It has taken another six years to find out what has happened to our daughter. To know it now—it is like this one pinprick of brightness on the dark map of Inara's past and future, like the name of a town.

That beautiful, bright dot.

And because of that dot, because the whole exome sequencing on Inara and the other nine children has made it possible to identify what has happened to her genetic code, other parents in the future may not have to stagger so long in the dark, as we did. They can be told what the syndrome is, what causes it, that it can be survived (though it is dangerous), and that it does not get progressively worse over time. That is Inara's gift to the world—the gift of knowledge and hope to the parents of other children like her. That is why I am crying right now, as I write.

_____

Those who've read my novel *What Our Eyes Have Witnessed* will be acquainted with my love for the Φῶς ἱλαρον (the *Phos hilaron*), one of the earliest recorded Christian hymns outside of the New Testament, dating back to the third century. It is in Greek, and it is a lovely and beautiful song. If you would like to hear a particularly breathtaking rendition in English with female vocals, look up the Cambridge Chorale performance of Owain Park's composition for the song at Ely Cathedral; at the time of my writing, that performance is available on youtube here:

www.youtube.com/watch?v=Xlemfvr_GaY

It is just two and a half minutes long. The *Phos hilaron* was a very brief hymn, probably intended to be easy for people to remember and sing each day. The hymn opens like this:

Φῶς ἱλαρον

Phos hilaron: O joyous light! The first thing you need to know is that this was a sunset hymn, sung at the last moment of day and the first moment of dusk—and also at the lighting of candles. At the onset of night, this hymn—*O joyous light!*—was sung by slaves and homeowners both, by women and men, by children and elders, and by people so impoverished they didn't know if they would have bread to eat the next day. It was sung at times by people in hiding, unsure if they might be arrested during the dark of night. It was sung while the day died and while, in Homer's phrase, "the roads of the world grew dark." It was sung in the hope that the sun (and the Son) would come back and give light again to the world. Many of us might take it for granted that our earth will turn her face to the sun again at dawn, but not all of these people could take it for granted that they'd be there to see it. At the hospital, and after, *I* could not take it for granted that my daughter would see the next dawn, or that I would see another morning with her. Perhaps, for me, as for the people who first sang the *Phos hilaron* long ago, the roads of the world would *stay* dark. That was a possibility. And as the sun sank, as I anxiously watched Inara's tachychardic heart rate on the monitor, as I watch a machine do her breathing for her—through an intubated tube—I did not know if Inara would make it to the other side of the night. I could only hope, fiercely, unstoppably, because she needed me to. Because she needed me at her side, her dad, believing in her. And perhaps, Inara needed the kind of dad who would glance at the hospital window at the last failing light of the day and whisper, or sing, or shout, "O joyous light!" even as it vanished from the world, hoping against all hope both that it would return and that my daughter's eyes would be open and alive to see it.

The old song continues:

ἁγιας δοξης αθανατου Πατρος,
ουρανιου, ἁγιου, μακαρος,

—*hagias doxes athanatou Patros, ouraniou, hagiou, makaros*—O joyous light of the undying glory of the Father, heavenly, holy, blessed. A song sung at evening to remind us that the sun's light is undying and the Father's is, too. *Athanatos,* undying. What a hope! What a ridiculous, beautiful hope. *Ouraniou*: heavenly—something not just up in the sky but all around us, all around this earth, surrounding it—and us— on all sides. Contrary to what some elementary schools used to teach about Christopher Columbus discovering the roundness of the world, the ancient Greeks were well aware that the earth hung in the heavens like a pendant orb, and that the cosmos surrounded us on all sides. Granted, they thought that the earth was at the center of the cosmos, but they were under no illusion that the Earth was some type of flat disc with a bowl of sky. When second-century worshippers sang *ouraniou*, they knew that heaven was not only above but surrounding us, all about us, immanently present, in the air we breathe, in the stars high over our heads, in the stars far beneath our feet that we cannot see.

Hagiou, holy. The word really means apart, distinct, different. As the sun in the sky is distinct and apart from our lived experience, something high and untouchable yet something that gives life and heat—so too did they imagine the Father, holy and apart. And that was cause for hope, not a delicate hope but a sword-in-the-hand hope, the kind of hope that gets you through the night. Though at night your mortal eyes can see neither our native star nor the heavenly Father, you can still remember them. You can unforget that there is something *more* than the pain and suffering you endure, or that your children endure. That what you see is not all there is, and that there is meaning beyond the exigencies and terrors of the present moment.

There is a scene in J.R.R. Tolkien's *The Return of the King* that steals my heart. Sam and Frodo are crossing the wastes of Mordor, and they have stopped for the night. It has been days since either of them has seen sunlight. The air smells of sulphur and smoke, and they are hunted. The weight of the world is on their shoulders, and they cannot see a clear path to achieving their mission, nor to survival after it. During that longest night, Sam Gamgee glances up:

> There, peeping among the cloud-wrack above a dark tor high up in the mountains, Sam saw a white star twinkle for a while. The beauty of it smote his heart, as he looked up out of the forsaken land, and hope returned to him. For like a shaft, clear and cold, the thought pierced him that in the end the Shadow was only a small and passing thing: there was light and high beauty for ever beyond its reach.

J.R.R. TOLKIEN, *THE RETURN OF THE KING*

There with Sam, as a reader, I am breathless at that beauty he sees in the sky, a light in dark places when all other lights go out. It is a *Phos hilaron* moment. O joyous light. For Sam, that light, that star, is *hagios*; it is holy and hallowed, set apart from the woes of this middle earth on which we walk and in which, at times, we suffer. It offers momentary and visible proof that this suffering is not all there is, that this fear is not the totality of our experience. Once the clouds and smoke and battle-wrack hide that star again, Sam will not have such visible proof, but he will retain the dream and the memory of it, and the ability to sing of the light he cannot see.

Did you ever read *The Silver Chair* by C. S Lewis? In it, one of the most beautiful statements of hope that I have ever read is expressed by Puddleglum—taciturn, morose, stick-in-the-mud, always-expecting-the-worst, chronically worried, practical, loyal Puddleglum. When a witch in an underground kingdom (a place of horrors) tells a spell-struck Puddleglum and the children that they have only ever imagined that there was another world above ground, and grass, and clean good air, and a *sun*, and a lion named Aslan, Puddleglum says:

Suppose we have only dreamed, or made up, all those things—trees and grass and sun and moon and stars and Aslan himself. Suppose we have. Then all I can say is that, in that case, the made-up things seem a good deal more important than the real ones. Suppose this black pit of a kingdom of yours is the only world. Well, it strikes me as a pretty poor one. And that's a funny thing, when you come to think of it. We're just babies making up a game, if you're right. But four babies playing a game can make a play-world which licks your real world hollow. That's why I'm going to stand by the play world. I'm on Aslan's side even if there isn't any Aslan to lead it. I'm going to live as like a Narnian as I can even if there isn't any Narnia. So, thanking you kindly for our supper, if these two gentlemen and the young lady are ready, we're leaving your court at once and setting out in the dark to spend our lives looking for Overland.

C.S. LEWIS, *THE SILVER CHAIR*

Bless you, Puddleglum. This passage is his *Phos hilaron*, his cry of *O joyous light!* even while he expects to molder in the dark. It is a strong hope, a defiant hope, an unstoppable hope, a hope that doesn't count the cost of walking on the water, a hope that bids you just step out of the boat and *walk*, with the ensorcelled children in your arms, because that is what you *do*. You live like a Narnian even if there isn't any Narnia. You hope the sun will come back and you keep walking in the dark and *you don't stop*.

O joyous light.

Makaros—blessed—the hymn continues. *Blessed* Father. The Father made big, his name made great in all the earth. The Father who makes *us* big by his love. Who teaches us to make others big by *our* love.

ουρανιου, ἁγιου, μακαρος,

Ouraniou, hagiou, makaros: heavenly, holy and distinct, blessed and embiggened. Puddleglum's hope is that the outer world is still all around is, if you can just dig your way up to it; that it is something distinct and beautiful and *more* than what you can see down here in the dark; and that it is *big*. Believing in that bigness makes his heart big, so that he throws off the spell—not because the spell of despair doesn't act upon his mind but because it isn't the *only* thing that does; it isn't the only thing that can, even in the dark, even in terror, even after the sun has set. His defiant hope is a *big* hope.

So is mine. My Inara has taught me such big hope.

I waited long and long, in the dark. But O joyous light.

The song goes on to name Father, Son, and Spirit—it is a very early Trinity hymn—and then it breaks into this:

αξιον σε εν πασι καιροις ὑμνεισθαι φωναις αισιαις,

Axion se en pasi kairois hymneisthai phonais aisiais: Meet it is at all times to worship you with voices of praise. When is it appropriate to hope? When is hope *right?* The song's answer to this is: At all times, in all seasons, because when you live lives of unstoppable hope, all seasons are *kairoi*, every night is a *kairos*—an opportune time, the "right moment" when anything can happen, when a miracle can occur or an epiphany be glimpsed, when something can visit you in the dark, some knowledge or experience or unexpected gift that might upend or rewrite or reinterpret your life and your story. It is *always* the right time, even and especially when the roads of the world grow dark.

Υιε Θεου, ζωην ὁ διδους, διο ὁ κοσμος σε δοξαζει.

Hyie Theou, zoen ho didous, dio ho kosmos se doxazei: O son of God and Life Giver, therefore the universe glorifies you. The song is pure hope. It doesn't lay out doctrine (though it alludes to it); it doesn't retell the narrative of the gospel, but it shares its very heart, which is hope. All the song says is: *The sun is going down. We are singing to the glorious light, because it is right to sing in the dark. Because it is the right time to sing with joy, therefore the universe gives you glory, Life Giver.*

That hits at my heart. Logicians would call it a tautology, a circular argument: This is the right time to hope, because this is the time when we are hoping. But the hymn doesn't care about arguments. It deals neither in doctrine nor logical propositions, but in the simple, emotive expression of defiance and joy: defiance at the dark and joy at the light, even when you can't see it, even when the dark appears to be all there is and its victory seems certain and imminent. This hymn, this early and ancient hymn that was sung eighteen hundred years ago, could have said instead: *We know the sun will be back; therefore we will persist until it returns.* Or it could have said, *The sun has always returned after a long night before; therefore we will wait during this night too.* But the song doesn't bother to say any of that. It's not trying to persuade you or convince you or compel you. It's just a *song*, a shout, a cry in the night: *It is too dark to see, but O joyous light! We hope, we hope, we hope.*

It is the song of people who don't know if they'll make it and who intend, fiercely, joyously, to make it nonetheless. It is the song of people living blessed lives, unstoppable lives.

It is a *good* song.

———————

Inara's past six years have been filled with adventure, for we live in a time when girls in wheelchairs can explore the world too. So Inara rolled along the edge of the Grand Canyon, gazing across an ocean of air; she giggled at the flash of sunlight on the bluer-than-blue surface of deep Crater Lake in Oregon, at the top of a dead volcano; she played at sunset on the slope of a vast dune at the Great Sand Dunes National Park in Colorado, tracing her own patterns in the sand and letting it sift through her fingers; she let the waves kiss her toes on a gray and lonely Pacific beach; she sat in her chair inside one of the redwoods in the Muir forest, one

of the cathedral trees, hollowed out by the fires of centuries past yet still growing strong and hale, as she is. There, wrapped in a ladybug blanket, was Inara, tiny—unlikely ever to reach five feet in height—and young, sitting *inside* the largest and most ancient living organism I had ever encountered, a tree a thousand years old and tall enough to touch the sky. And she giggled.

She has traveled to Evermore, too—an amusement park in Utah designed for live-action roleplaying in a fantasy town, replete with elves, fairies, mages, and ghouls. Inara rolled happily along in the evil dark between flickering torches in the catacombs beneath a church, and when the unquiet dead came lurching out at her, she laughed herself silly. She even tried to grab hold of their shrouded limbs herself. Possibly our little dragon wanted a bite. She laughed, too, at the towering puppet that was the Elder King, as he lifted his arms and boomed and menaced the gathered villagers. Inara's eyes shone with mischief, as if she wanted to say, *Hello brother, I am fiercer than you.* She bounced in her chair to the rhythm of musicians inside a tavern fashioned like a hobbit hole, and she rolled through a corn maze, bumpity bump, one punctuated by giant pumpkins, while distant werewolves howled at the harvest moon.

I took her to Dinosaur Ridge, too, so that she could touch the bones of brontosaurs and peer at giant sauropod footprints from beneath. Being a little dragon herself, she needed to see the remains of her distant cousins.

Sometimes on these journeys she seemed wistful, as if she might want to chase other children running along the paths, but most often she looked amused, as she frequently does, as though she is convinced God has arranged this odd,

119

half-visible world as a personal entertainment and jest for
her enjoyment. She is hitting puberty now and at times has
dark moods and rages that could put a mythical barbarian
to shame, and she hurls things in her room and creates a
tempest of crashing and screams, but these pass swiftly. Her
more usual mode of interacting with her world is glee and
mischief. In either mood, she lives her life with a vivacity
and voracity that her mother and I envy and hope to
emulate when we can.

She is a terrible flirt. Before the pandemic, she would
attend hippotherapy once every other week. That has
nothing to do with hippopotamuses but with horses; the
word is Greek for *horse healing* (and "hippopotamus" is *river
horse*). This involves lifting Inara into a saddle and having
her ride a horse while a couple of volunteers—typically
strapping young Catholic lads from nearby Regis
University—walk beside the animal to either side. The
rolling gait of the horse and the necessity of keeping balance
teaches Inara to use the muscles she needs for walking, and
since beginning hippotherapy, her mobility has increased
dramatically. She can now walk *very fast* when she intends to,
by the simple device of hurling herself forward and catching
herself just in time, before falling. We all do that when we
walk—throw ourselves forward and catch ourselves;
bipedal, heel-to-toe walking is just controlled falling, a kind
of constant defiance of gravity. We are basically all just
showing off when we walk. Inara just does it with less
balance and more vigor.

Hippotherapy afternoons were her favorite. Though she
had become quite mobile, as soon as "the Regis boys"
would show up, Inara would get a sly look in her eye, giggle,
and then swoon rather dramatically, pretending to be limp

and helpless and at risk of sliding right off the horse at any moment. In fact, she often would slide out of the saddle, timing it just right for one of the Regis boys to catch her. She would reward him with an adoring look and a snuggle. As her mother had often seen her ride with quiet competence and confidence when they weren't present, and as we had both seen her rip apart a room at home in less time than it takes to sneeze, we observed this swooning with quiet amusement. Because we are in the midst of a global pandemic at the time of writing this, Inara has not seen her Regis boys in a year. I think she misses them.

In the same spirit of mischief, Inara is also a skilled pickpocket. While wheeling her chair through a press of people, she will reach, quite sneakily, and slip a wallet from a pocket or, more frequently, a smartphone, which we must then figure out how to return. Her ILC (Independent Learning Classroom) teacher has lost his phone to her countless times. With people like him—people she knows—she will slyly go in for a snuggle and then pluck the phone from your pocket while you're distracted. The objective of this game of Artful Dodger, of course, is to chew on the phone.

So life with Inara is always eventful, packed with laughter and with groans of chagrin. We are currently working on installing a new wall and a door at the top of the stairs to the basement, because our cortically blind yet now more-mobile child, who often staggers about the house without need or desire for her chair, is absolutely determined to take "flying lessons" and chuck herself down the stairs, for the sheer mischievous fun of it. Less fun for *us*—we are high-strung enough as it is. To survive as a parent in our household, some degree of wild gallows humor is required.

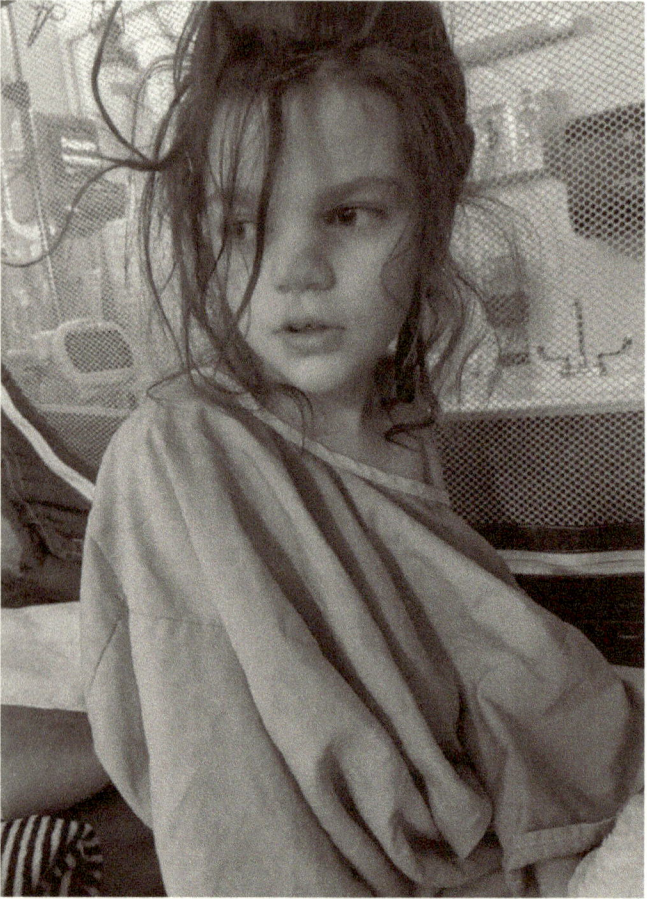

It is not the stairs that terrify me, however; I am already hyper-vigilant enough to keep my daughter away from a stairwell. No, it is the seizures, which, when they come,

come in rapid clusters, until her body is seizing without cease, and parts of her body simply stop working.

My persistent fear, the fear that grips my heart, is that a seizure could take Inara away from us in an hour; between dusk and dawn on any night, unpredictably, we could lose her. That is why I sing *Phos hilaron*. That is why I devote each precious moment to her that I can. These moments are blessed. They are brief, but they are big.

I do not know which specific hopes to hold for Inara's future, because often my primary hope—that for her survival—beats so strongly in my heart that it drowns out all else. And also, as I have only known for a few days *what* her condition actually is, I have spent the last nine years without any clear expectations or anything to base expectations on. I have had to learn to take each day as it comes, celebrating the moments with Inara that I have, laughing with her or crying with her as the particular occasion demands. My wife believes that Inara will one day speak, make great art, and even marry, if she wishes. Or that she will live with us for as long as we prove physically able to care for her, and that we will do our best to leave behind a fund for her care. We decided to have a third child—our delightful son Círdan Leto Litore—both so that Inara's care would not one day fall entirely on one sibling; so that River, her older sister, would get to experience having a sibling who could be a more talkative companion and more active playmate; and so that Inara herself could experience being an older sister. We know now that some children with a mutation in RHOBTB2 do learn to speak one or two-word utterances. Our Inara is, so far, nonverbal, but she understands much of what is said to her, and she does have a vocabulary of ninety-eight utterances and sounds that are each attached to distinct feelings, objects, or people; she makes a different sound when greeting her mother, when greeting me, and when greeting her para, for instance. There is a distinct possibility that she may one day have a similar vocabulary of single words, as well. Or, she may build a vocabulary of sign, or she might master some assistive device that speaks for her. There are many roads into the future, and for nine years it has been impossible to draw a map because no one knew the name of the town where our journey started. Now, we are at least to write RHOBTB2 on the map as an origin point, but as we are among the first to document a journey from that origin point to anywhere else, we don't really know clearly what's ahead, only that we are no longer the only ones walking on the road. Whatever skills and abilities Inara may come to possess, her trajectory is at least forward, *that way,* through the dark forest, leveling up as she goes. She is a keenly intelligent little adventurer, and creative, and yes, destructive too. She will have setbacks along the way, when she seizes. If they are as violent as those that put her on a helicopter rushing to our state's leading hospital a few weeks ago, they may erase some of her progress, for a time. The left side of her body is now very weak; she has less balance, less control of her left leg and foot. Before her recent seizures, we saw her climb on top of the dining room table, hurl everything on it to the floor, lift her head, and screech like a tyrannosaur declaring its victory over the ancient prairie; she can no longer do that. But, through aggressive physical therapy and her own indomitable will, she will get it back. And that is how it will go. If she has several years without seizures—as she did before this January—she will gain skills and mobility. When she seizes severely, she will lose some. But, if she lives, she will get it back. She will keep staggering, or stumbling, or perhaps one day running, through that wild forest that is her uncharted life. And whatever comes, I believe that she will overcome it and screech like a tyrannosaur once she has. And I hope, I hope with my whole heart, with all my strength, with all my fiercest determination to accompany her—I hope that one day, she and her siblings will bury her mother and me in the quiet earth, and that we will not bury her.

We live, my wife and I, with the awareness of mortality, always. It isn't something we can hide from, as many people used to, I think, in the days before the COVID-19 pandemic. Life has a different taste and smell when you are acutely aware that at any moment, you might lose your loved ones. I don't know how else to speak of it.

But hope feels different now too, because it also is something we carry with us at all times, like an implement we stand ready to wield—like a sorcerer's staff or a samurai's katana. More than a tool, it has become a part of us, a part of how we exist in our world, a way of sleeping in our armor.

Inara in her moment of triumph. The floors are hardwood, to help her keep her balance and navigate the house. The table too, evidently.

One of the geneticists we spoke with said that twelve years ago, if a child had epilepsy, there were only two genes we were able to test for. By the time we tested Inara at three years of age, there were two hundred and fifty. Now there are more, and RHOBTB2 is being added to that library. That means that untold numbers of children who have symptoms like Inara can now be tested for her condition. This makes a tremendous difference in the quality of care that can be provided to such children.

To cite just one example, Inara is, well, tiny. She fell off her growth chart a *long* time ago. Do you know Shakespeare's line, from *A Midsummer Night's Dream?*

"Though she be but little she is fierce"

That is our Inara Cahira. Her physicians have pushed us to increase her feeds (she is still nourished primarily by a gastronomy tube, with liquid food pumped directly into her belly at meals), and she has been diagnosed from time to time with "failure to thrive" due to being extremely undersized. Yet her energy level is high, and when her feeds are increased, she can't keep them down; her stomach becomes upset and she vomits—which in turn increases her risk for seizures.

Now that we know about RHOBTB2, we know that Inara's tiny size isn't the abnormality or sign of frailty that it appears; it's normal for children with her condition. They are *all* small. That's one of the consequences of this error in genetic coding; much expected growth simply doesn't occur. Often, children with RHOBTB2 have smaller heads, as well, something that becomes proportionally more apparent as they age. Small size, big heart, big attitude: that's our Inara. And now that we know this, the doctors can help us make more informed decisions than before about her diet, her caloric intake, and her gastrointestinal health. We are less likely to be advised to dangerously overfeed her in the desire to cure an assumed frailty. We can instead tailor her feed to her condition and her particular needs—an easier thing to do when you know *what* her condition is.

That's just one example. It is why I have such joy that parents whose infants suffer as Inara did can get tested for RHOBTB2 and can receive help and advice early. That is exciting. And—for myself—this new knowledge tastes very sweet. There is a weight lifting from my shoulders that has been there so long, I had forgotten I was carrying it.

Knowledge can make a fitting sheath for the sword of hope, or perhaps knowledge is the shield we hold strapped to the other arm as we venture and adventure in this dark wood. I love those passages in the Psalms when readers are advised to *consider* this world God has made; we lose so much in translation, both because of deep differences between the tone, mood, and grammar of Hebrew and that of English, and because of the strain of anti-intellectualism in our American culture that runs so profoundly counter to the Hebrew longing for wisdom that permeates the Tanakh and the Old Testament. The word we translate *consider* doesn't mean to look up at the sky or at the world or at the workings of the human body and just marvel mutely at it; it means to see deeply into, to diligently observe and attend to, to glory in learning what is around us and inside us. Similarly there is a prayer in the Quran, where the faithful person cries, "Lord, enrich me with knowledge!" That, and other passages in the Quran about seeking knowledge, I have adapted often in my science fiction series *Ansible* (about twenty-fifth century Islamic intergalactic explorers and time travelers), paraphrased this way:

> *Gather knowledge:*
> *Knowledge is our companion in the night land,*
> *Our shield against terrors.*

The psalmist tells us that we are fearfully and wonderfully made, and that this is matter for rejoicing. While the Scriptures do caution that human wisdom is rarely sufficient, that God alone is sufficient, they also urge us, repeatedly, to yearn for wisdom as young Solomon did and as the Queen of Sheba did, crossing a continent for a conversation with another learned mind, and to study avidly as Jeremiah, Paul, and Mary sister of Martha did. The Scriptures emphasize that we are made with hearts and minds that cry out for knowledge. When we scorn the pursuit of knowledge, we mock our Maker.

In Genesis, we are given the story of Babel, of humans divided and separated by divisions in speech, but in this latter day, we have been granted access to a shared language again: DNA. The base code of life. The programming language in which our very bodies and minds are written. Not so that we can build a tower in affront to heaven, but so that we can read the book of life in its own language—read, understand, and learn it together—and in so doing, learn more about ourselves and about other life on our planet. In doing this, we glorify our Creator and heal many wounds.

Inara's siblings River and Círdan, growing so fast. Reading so much.

River's favorite thing in the world right now is coding. She is in fifth grade, and her school has provided a program that allows her to define variables and simple commands that trigger particular choices of color, music, and dance for cartoonish figures on the computer screen. In addition, I've shown her ren.py, which is a free, open source coding program for creating visual novels and choose your own adventure stories. She revels in it; it requires her to learn and use a rudimentary coding language—and she also gets to learn how to debug her code.

Her mother and I have had some thrilling conversations with River about *genetic* code, about that code that is more complex by far than the four hundred lines of programming River has just written and run. If you were to stretch out your entire DNA code into a single thread, it would be the length of seventy voyages from the earth to the sun and back. That's a lot of code. Each human being you encounter this week is a living text more vast than any library on Earth. To my thinking, that makes the untimely death of any human being all the more tragic, and the survival of any human being all the more beautiful. There is a proverb that when an old person dies, a library burns down, because we are each libraries of memory and experience; we are each libraries of code, too. We are each unthinkably blessed and big, even as we are at the same time remarkably small and fragile, as well. Each of us passing through this dark wood is a walking library, and we walk surrounded by beautiful, unpredictable, vast libraries. And that is a hopeful thought.

I wonder if I am now babbling. I am so overcome by the news of what we have learned, of what geneticists have discovered after several years of reading Inara's unique genetic code. I am in awe, thinking of the many secrets and surprises hidden inside the books (the cells) in each of our genetic libraries, each of our bodies.

This is what I have wanted to say.

A week ago, I was closer to despair than I have ever been. This most recent vigil in the hospital with Inara had shaken me to my foundation. Think of it: we'd had several years in which Inara's condition was controlled, in which she thrived and grew and *learned*. Until she could stand on a table! My friends and readers, that promise you make in your heart—that *the worst is now behind us*—that is a powerful drug. A comforting one. Maybe even a dangerous one, to some degree. Because then, in a single night, that promise was dashed to pieces like glass against a rock. In a single night, we plummeted through a slew of moments when her body *stopped*. And once we had her home again, she could barely stand. She had lost so much. She is already gaining it back, as quickly as she can. But, when I saw how much she had lost, and how easily she might still be taken from us, even after all the battles we'd fought and all the battles she'd won, even years after I thought that fear was now just a story in our past—that shook me. It dried me out, dried me of *everything* until I was too desiccated even for tears. I was still standing, still walking, because that is what I *do*. I had to be strong for my wife, who was exhausted; for River, who was terrified for her sister; for Círdan, who is only three and needs his parents attentive and present; for myself; and for my God, who bids me stand.

There were many things that helped me stand: Inara's giggles. River's fierce love of learning. Little Círdan's love (do you know, when Inara was lethargic after the night's seizures, Círdan *climbed onto her face* first thing that morning and showed us how unresponsive she was, so that we hit panic mode and rushed her to the ER). And the support and love of many friends, our wider family who are with us at heart, even though in a time of pandemic they cannot be with us in person. One friend, a writer, mailed Inara a plushie dunkleosteus, a giant prehistoric fish with jaws to rival our young dragon's. The original beast was thirty feet

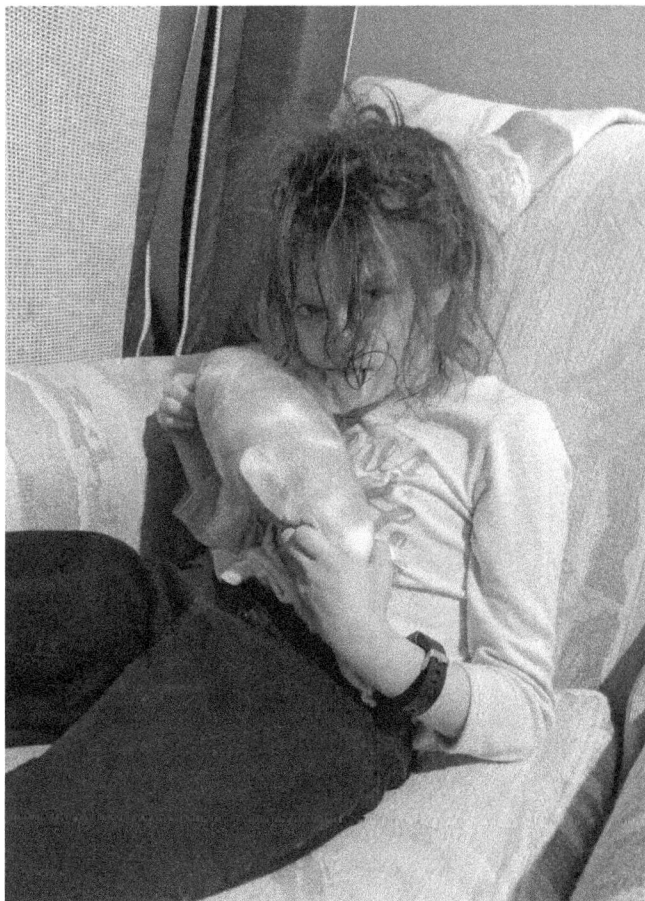

Prehistoric titan (Dunkleosteus) meets contemporary dragon.

long and armored, a leviathan of the Devonian world. Seeing Inara gnaw happily on her dunkleosteus, I remembered that I could smile.

But I could not find my blade, my hope. It wasn't that my blade had broken; I just didn't know where it *was*. I knew myself disarmed, beset, at risk of being lost in the dark. I held Inara tightly and thought, *I don't know how to keep you safe, and I don't know how to hope for your safety.*

And so I did the only thing I could: I just held her.

———

And now I have hope again. Maybe it was never a blade at all, just a worn, heavy longcoat against the lethal cold and a pair of gauntlets or steel-braced gloves, so that I can clear brush that's in our way as we walk.

———

Inara herself has given me that hope. Not because she, who cannot speak, can somehow promise me she will survive or be safe. And not because I am any more able now to protect her, my daughter who I love, than I was a few weeks ago. But simply because she has made this gift to the world. In reading the library that is Inara—or at least, a number of chapters in it—researchers have learned something that will help so many children. Whatever comes, whatever awaits us in the forest or across the waves we're walking on, Inara's life has had tremendous meaning.

And that reminded me of everything *else* that is so tremendously meaningful in her life, everything that I've written about here, and more, everything that I can hold near my heart: her laughter, her painting, her love of music (especially death metal, Inara being Inara), the look in her eyes when she felt the wind in her face at the brink of the Grand Canyon. Her screech of triumph when she stood on that table, momentarily empress and conqueror of her world.

Even if I lose her tonight, even if this is the last evening I sing her a lullaby or hold her before bed, all those experiences will have *been*, all those moments that are hers will have happened. Nothing can ever change that. She is Inara, living a life blessed and big. Looking back at all those moments behind us and at all the moments *today*, in this very hour, and knowing them for how beautiful they are, I can hope for many more. I can hold her close and whisper, *O joyous light.*

———————

In celebration of our family, Inara's big sister River and I are working, bit by bit, on making a book. I don't know yet if it will be a hardcover book that you can set on a table, or a ren.py visual novel that anyone can easily download; maybe the latter, so more people can read it. It's about being siblings, and it's a book for teaching young children about epilepsy. It's called *The Dragon in the Amazing Flying Wheelchair*, and in it, a ladybug (that's River) meets a dragon (that's Inara) who can't fly. Ladybug finds Dragon weeping beneath a tree and asks her what's wrong. River drew me this quick sketch of the scene:

From that point, the story goes like this:

"Ladybug! Ladybug!" Dragon cries. "I can't fly."

"Why not?" Ladybug asks.

"Well, I have epilepsy. I get seizures. I shake and shake and shake. And some parts of my body don't work like yours. Like my wings. They won't flap and lift me into the air."

Ladybug feels sad. "I wish you could fly up here with me," she says.

"I wish I could, too," Dragon says. And at that very moment, she has another seizure:

She shook and shook and shook. She couldn't control her body for five whole minutes. Ladybug worried about her friend and stayed close, to keep her safe. She stayed with her friend until the seizure was over.

When Dragon stopped shaking, she was very tired. Ladybug landed on her head. She kept her voice gentle and soft. She wanted to comfort her friend. "Dragon, what happened?" Ladybug asked.

"I had a seizure."

"I don't understand," Ladybug said. "What's a seizure?"

"Well," said Dragon, "you know how sometimes you get really, really excited, and you jump up and down or twirl around in circles?"

"Yes!" Ladybug got excited and jumped up in the air. "I do that lots!"

"Sometimes," said Dragon, "my brain gets excited, and it jumps up and down inside my head! And then my whole body shakes. It's called a seizure. And sometimes, if I get too many seizures, it's why I can't walk very far ... or fly."

"Oh no," Ladybug said. "Your brain is too excited to fly?"

Dragon nodded her head sadly. "Yes. My brain is very excited. All the time. It bounces around inside my head, just like a little kid that won't go to sleep." She gazed up at the sky and sighed. "My brain needs a nap. And I need to fly!"

And just at that moment, Ladybug had an idea.

And it wasn't just a good idea; it was a *great* idea. It was the *best* idea.

"Dragon!" she cried. "Don't go anywhere! Stay right here! I'll be right back! I promise!"

And she flew as fast as sunlight to go make her idea happen!—because when you have a great idea, when you have the *best* idea, there is no time to waste!

Ladybug had thought of something to build for her friend. Ladybug was the best at building things.

The story continues. Ladybug rushes to her friend Narwhal (that's little Círdan) to enlist his help, because while Ladybug is the best at building things, Narwhal is the best at *finding* things. Through many pages of trial and error, they manage to assemble the materials needed to bring Ladybug's idea to fruition.

Dragon doesn't realize what they're building, and she wonders wistfully what *she* might be best at. She realizes that even though she can't fly, there are many things that she, uniquely, can do. For example, she can light a fire with her breath, so that she and her friends Ladybug and Narwhal can toast marshmallows:

> Narwhal put one plump marshmallow on his long tusk. Dragon and Ladybug used sticks to roast theirs.

"These are *so good*!" Ladybug said.

"Tastiest marshmallows *ever*!" Narwhal said.

Dragon smiled. Her heart felt warm and good, and her tummy felt warm and full of gooey, yummy marshmallows. She had found something else she could be the best at. She was the best at making fires to roast marshmallows in!

(As it happens, Dragon also proves to be the best at igniting the toe hairs of abusive local giants who threaten to squash her friends and their project.)

As the story progresses, it turns out that what Narwhal has been finding are supplies for an ambitious feat of engineering (you can find *anything* in the underwater junkyards we've made of our seas, if you just look long enough), and what Ladybug has been building is a flying wheelchair. "Surprise!" she cries.

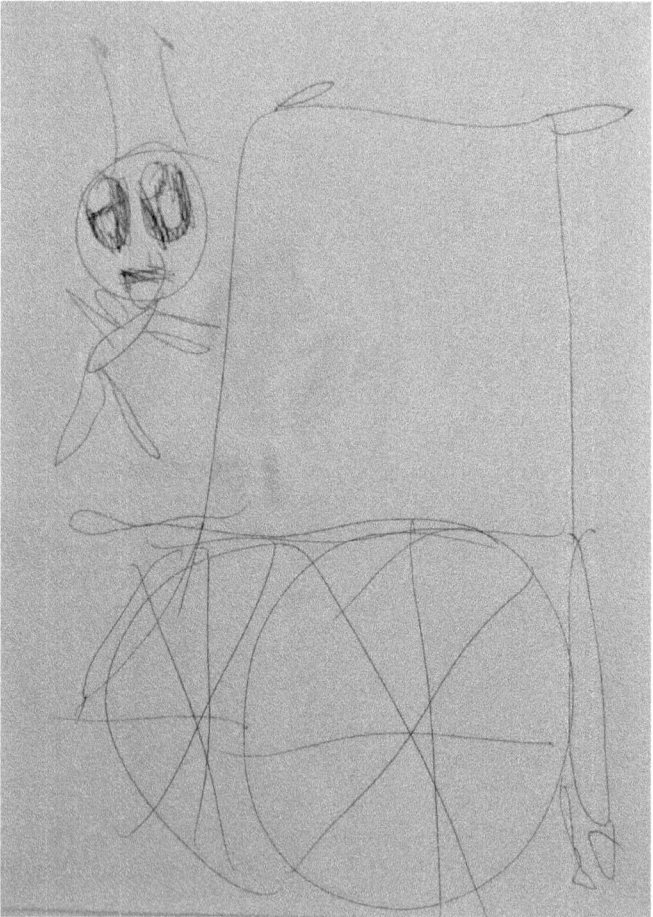

River had such fun imagining this flying wheelchair. "Look, Daddy!" she cried. "It has a *rocket launcher!*"

And so it does.

"What did Dragon think of the wheelchair?" I asked her.

Dragon was so excited!

"It's so ... so ... *wow!*" Dragon shouted happily. "My new wheelchair is completely, absolutely, positively *wow!* It's full of *wow!*"

As we near the end of the book, Dragon ignites the wheelchair's rocket with her fiery breath and roars high above mountains and castles, above bullying giants and wild seas and gentle forests. She can fly at last.

> When the sun set and it started to grow dark, Dragon zoomed her wheelchair back home. She landed on the grass and rolled its wheels right over to the big rock by the water, where Ladybug and Narwhal were waiting for her.
>
> "You are the best friends ever," Dragon said.
>
> That night, Dragon lit a fire, and the wheelchair glowed a little in the firelight. Narwhal found a bag of marshmallows floating on the water, Ladybug put the marshmallows on sticks, and they roasted them and ate s'mores. They were the best s'mores Ladybug, Dragon, and Narwhal had ever tasted.

We will finish that book when we can, likely with full color art by River. It isn't really a story about miracles or even problem-solving contraptions. It's a story about hope—and joy. About the joy we take in each other, and the beautiful moments—the marshmallows and s'mores—that we make together. And it's a story about standing up for each other, too.

It's the kind of story River loves to tell, a story of fun times with her brother and sister, and of the ways that they help each other grow kinder, braver, and smarter. That's the family motto:

Always be brave,
Always be smart,
Always be kind.
And always do unto others
As you would have them do unto you.

It's the best advice Jessica and I know of, to give to our children.

And that is the kind of story *The Dragon in the Amazing Flying Wheelchair* is, the kind River loves best.

I like it, too.

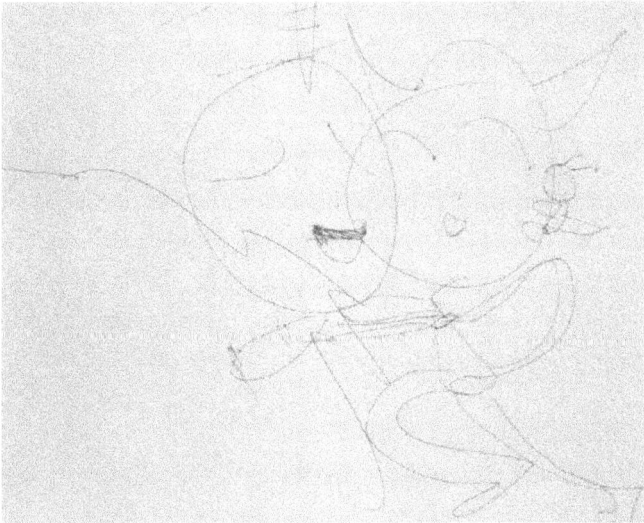

There they are: Ladybug, Dragon, and Narwhal. In River's words, "Friends forever."

If Inara had been telling this tale instead, it would more likely have been a yarn about a dragon laying waste to the countryside, thrashing her head to the tune of "Down with the Sickness," turning a line of poplars into matchsticks, cooking giants instead of marshmallows, and then laughing herself sick.

And probably that would make a good story, too.

So this week, I have learned to sing *Phos hilaron* again. May I never again forget, even for a moment.

Our lives are frail, but they are big, too. They are blessed. By our choices and our love and our devotion to something larger than ourselves, our lives can bless the lives of others. That is something I hope none of us ever forget.

Inara is not the only child who has suffered this year. There has been a pandemic. We've lost people. I've lost people—dear and cherished friends who I will not see again in this mortal life. We may lose more people yet. Earlier in the pandemic year, I wrote a tale about people who lose some of their kin before the onset of winter, to a devastating red rain that falls from the sky of their planet:

> On the first winter night after rainfall, when the humming people have gathered again in hiding … each person sings their tale of someone who didn't make it, someone the rain took. And all the stories of those who survived the red rain and those who didn't are braided together in one telling that night.

THE DAKOTARAPTOR RIDERS

I hope *we* will find ways to braid our tales and our lives together too. The red rain has fallen, and the world is colder now, and I fear continually for my Inara. This lonely winter, I feel frail, and I am very tired. But however fatigued, I will keep walking on the water with my Lord and with my dragon daughter—however cold the waves, however dark the night, however hidden the stars may be above an obscuring hellscape of smoke and volcanic fire. Since I have no map and have only *just* learned the name of the town we are walking *from* (that town with the unimposing yet significant name of RHOBTB2), I can't be certain now if we're walking through Mordor or across the Sea of Galilee or under the winterbound trees of Narnia. I don't know *where* this is. But I hope I know what the sun is (and what the Son is), and so I sing, *O joyous light*, even when I can't see that light, even when I am not sure I can rightly remember it, because I yearn for it nonetheless, and I yearn to reach that other shore. I yearn for us to reach it together.

Once upon a time, I carried my daughter with me in my arms while walking across this water. Now she staggers along beside me, off balance, laughing herself giddy, waving a hand at the roar of the waves or at the howling of wind in the trees, deeply amused. I am … *less* amused, but her laughter cheers me.

Maybe, while you have read this book, her laughter has cheered you, too. In either case, let us walk with each other in the dark in such a way that none of us need walk alone. Sing with me, if you can. And if you can't, I will sing and Inara will roar and screech for both of us, for as long as it takes to get to the other side of this night:

147

Φως ἱλαρον ἁγιας δοξης αθανατου Πατρος,
ουρανιου, ἁγιου, μακαρος,

Phos hilaron hagias doxes athanatou Patros,
ouraniou, hagiou, makaros,

O joyous light of the undying glory of the Father,
heavenly, holy, blessed.

It's a midnight forest through which we travel, a dark sea
over which we journey. I know only a very little of where
we're going. But I know who I'm going there with. And
there's hope in that.

After all, whatever the outcome, any journey undertaken
either with the Father or with my little Inara is likely to be
quite an adventure. One I'll be telling stories about, all my
life. I know your crossing of the water is quite the adventure,
too, a story bigger and more blessed than we are usually
brave enough (or unweary enough) to believe. And I am all
the more hopeful, knowing that as I walk here, the vast
library that is you walks nearby. Around us, there are all
these libraries striding toward the farther shore, waiting for
sunrise on the water, each of us so full of stories we could
burst. We have terror and we have grief, and yet this walk is
so beautiful. Sometimes, there is starlight on the water. Can
you see its beauty? Or if it's still dark as pitch and nothing
can be seen, can we sing of it? O joyous light!

Prayer

Father, it has been too long since I prayed. There is a wound in my heart. But there is also a road beneath my feet, and my daughter's small hand in mine. So here I kneel a moment. Father, I ask your blessing. I have a long journey ahead, and I know that I am not big enough for it. So bless me, Father, if it be your will—make me bigger, big enough for this road, big enough to walk beside my daughter, who looms to my left, such a magnificent, resplendent dragon. Maybe…even big enough to walk beside you. Make my heart big. Make my hope big. Forgive me for the nights when I have been too small. Small or big, frail or steady, I am here. And I love you, Father.

EPILOGUE:
DRAGONSCALE GLOVES

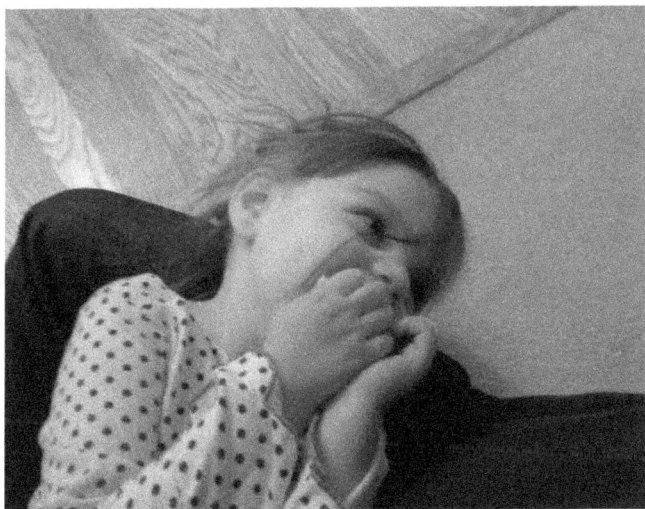

I DO NOT YET KNOW THE ENDING of the story in this book—neither the story of this study of the Beatitudes, nor the story of Inara—because I hope that both will go on a long time yet, and who can say what awaits us in the chapters yet to come? Nevertheless, I must end this book, because it has caught up with where *I* am at in the story. And I will end it with a request for your support. Inara's care can be expensive—and it can also be expensive to

153

transition, year by year, to a stay-at-home dad and caregiver for a disabled child and two siblings with challenges of their own (albeit not life-threatening ones). You have already helped considerably by buying this book; that itself has put a meal on our table. If you would like to help more, or if you would like to be a part of our story, here are three easy ways to do that.

One is to get a pair of dragonscale gloves, for yourself or a friend. Jessica makes them, and they are very beautiful. They are made in honor of Inara, our little dragon. They can be custom ordered here:

www.etsy.com/shop/seaelven

A second way to support is to join my Patreon, which is a membership community that funds my writing and helps keep this family cared for and fed. I believe passionately that storytelling is a communal act. Our ancestors sat around a fire sharing tales and giving each other chills. Patreon is a way to use modern-day patronage to achieve that again. It means taking writing fiction from something that just happens on a dining room table or in a basement study to something that happens around a community fire or a community table, with boisterous laughter and shared tears. And that's how it should be.

If you're the kind of reader who has always wished you could sit down on a porch with one of your favorite writers to just listen to the rain and ask them that question you've always had or even just hear them spin out new ideas, then you belong here. That's the kind of connection I want with my readers; that's the kind of connection I want with you. So I hope you'll consider joining me there:

www.patreon.com/stantlitore

The third way is to get more books. You can buy another copy of this one for a friend, or visit my direct store and explore other books about translating sacred texts or even some of my science fiction and fantasy, which I have been told provides quite a fierce entertainment by the winter fire:

https://stantlitore.itch.io/

I can also be reached by email at zombiebible@gmail.com.

I hope this book has moved you. I have told many stories over the years, and all of them are deeply personal to me, but this one more so than all the others, and Inara's story is the best story I have to tell.

May all of you live lives that are blessed and big, lives of unstoppable hope.

STANT LITORE
FEBRUARY 2021

ABOUT STANT LITORE

Stant Litore is the author of *Ansible: A Thousand Faces*, *The Zombie Bible*, and *The Dakotaraptor Riders*, as well as the nonfiction titles *On the Other Side of the Night* and *Lives of Unforgetting: What We Lose in Translation When We Read the Bible*. Best known for his weird fiction and scifi, he has taught frequent courses for writers, as well as religious studies courses for the Platt Park Church community. His fiction has been acclaimed by NPR, has served as the subject of scholarly work in *Relegere* and *Weird Fiction Review*, and he has been hailed as "SF's premier poet of loneliness." He lives in Colorado with his wife and three children, and is working on his next book.

www.ingramcontent.com/pod-product-compliance
Lightning Source LLC
Chambersburg PA
CBHW030835090426
42737CB00009B/981